Hot Topics 2

CHERYL PAVLIK

THOMSON

HEINLE ™

Austrialia • Canada • Mexico • Singapore • United Kingdom • United States

HOT TOPICS 2
by *Cheryl Pavlik*

Publisher, Adult and Academic ESL: *James W. Brown*
Senior Acquisitions Editor: *Sherrise Roehr*
Director of Product Development: *Anita Raducanu*
Development Editor: *Sarah Barnicle*
Editorial Assistants: *Katherine Reilly;*
      Bridget McLaughlin
Marketing Manager: *Laura Needham*
Senior Production Editor: *Maryellen Killeen*

Senior Print Buyer: *Mary Beth Hennebury*
Photo Researcher: *Melissa Goodrum*
Contributing Writer: *Hilary Grant*
Project Manager: *Tunde A. Dewey*
Compositor: *Parkwood Composition*
Text Printer/Binder: *Transcontinental Printing*
Cover and Interior Designer: *Lori Stuart*

Printed in Canada
1 2 3 4 5 6 7 8 9 10 08 07 06 05

For more information, contact Thomson/Heinle,
25 Thomson Place, Boston, MA 002210 USA, or you
can visit our Internet site at http://www.heinle.com

For permission to use material from this text or product,
contact us:
Tel   1-800-730-2214
Fax   1-800-730-2215
Web   www.thomsonrights.com

Library of Congress Control Number
2005921079

ISBN: 1-4130-0706-6

BRIEF CONTENTS

KEY   ⌇ = *warm*   ⌇⌇ = *hot*   ⌇⌇⌇ = *hotter*
⌇⌇⌇⌇ = *sizzling*   ⌇⌇⌇⌇⌇ = *scorching*

CONTENTS

* In addition to chapter-specific reading skills, each chapter includes exercises to practice the following skills: previewing, predicting, skimming, scanning, fact-finding, guessing meaning from related words, guessing meaning from context, word parts analysis, critical thinking, and discussion questions.

CONTENTS

* In addition to chapter-specific reading skills, each chapter includes exercises to practice the following skills: previewing, predicting, skimming, scanning, fact-finding, guessing meaning from related words, guessing meaning from context, word parts analysis, critical thinking, and discussion questions.

TO THE TEACHER

In the 30 years that I have been in English language training (ELT), I have despaired of the lack of stimulating reading texts, accompanied by activities written specifically to energize and inspire the mature English learner. Why aren't many ESL reading texts sufficient? Although ESL learners may not yet have mastered English syntax, they still have interests beyond the mundane, and they certainly have ample reasoning ability. And while many reading texts are written about subjects of broad appeal, virtually all of them avoid topics that are deemed "too controversial" for the classroom setting. Unfortunately, many of those neglected topics are of great interest and relevance to adult lives. By steering course themes away from controversy, the instructor also steers students away from motivating and stimulating topics.

Hot Topics 2 is different from other reading and discussion texts because it dares to deal with demanding subjects such as *violence* and *cultural ideas of beauty*. These topics have not been chosen to shock students, but merely to give them a chance to talk about matters that people discuss every day in their first language. That said, not every topic will be appropriate for every classroom. Some themes such as *intelligence* will probably be acceptable in any classroom. Others such as *gambling* or *infidelity* might prove problematic in some teaching situations. To assist, each chapter in the table of contents is rated by the amount of controversy it is likely to cause. Of course, teachers should read the articles in each chapter carefully and decide if their students would feel comfortable having a discussion on a particular topic. Another way to determine which chapters to use in class might be to have students look through the book and then vote on specific topics they are interested in reading and discussing. Even though the chapters at the beginning of each book are generally easier than the chapters at the end, the text has been designed so that chapters can be omitted entirely or covered in a different order.

Series Overview

Hot Topics is a three-level reading discussion series written for inquisitive, mature students of English language learners. Each chapter contains several high-interest readings on a specific controversial and thought-provoking topic.

Reading Selections

Each level of *Hot Topics* consists of 14 chapters. The readings in *Hot Topics* are crafted to present students with challenging reading material including some vocabulary that one might not expect to find in a low-level text. The reason for this is twofold. First, it is almost impossible to deal with these "hot" topics in a meaningful way without more sophisticated vocabulary. Second, and more importantly, it is ineffective to teach reading strategies using materials that provide no challenge. In the same way that one would not use a hammer to push in a thumbtack, readers do not need reading strategies when the meaning of a text is evident. Reading strategies are best learned when one *has to* employ them to aid comprehension.

Each chapter in the book is composed of two parts. Part I will contain two or three short readings on a topic. These readings are preceded by activities that help students make guesses about the genre, level, and content of the material they are going to read, activating their own schemata or bases of knowledge before reading the text. The readings are followed by extensive exercises that help students thoroughly analyze the content and the structure of the readings.

Part II consists of a single, more challenging reading. Although more difficult, the readings in Part II have direct topical and lexical connection to the readings in Part I. Research shows that the amount of background knowledge one has on a subject directly affects reading comprehension. Therefore, these readings will move the students to an even higher reading level by building on the concepts, information, and vocabulary that they have acquired in Part I. Complete comprehension of the text will not be expected, however. For some students this will prove a difficult task in itself. However, learning to cope with a less than full understanding is an important reading strategy— probably one of the most useful ones that nonnative readers will learn.

Chapter Outline and Teaching Suggestions

PART I

Preview

This section contains prereading questions, photographs, and/or activities that introduce the topic and some of the vocabulary. This section is best completed as group work or class discussion.

Predict

In this section, students are directed to look at certain features of the text(s) and then make predictions. These predictions include areas such as content, genre, level of difficulty, and reliability of the information.

Read It

This section is generally composed of two or three readings centered on a particular "hot" topic. In each reading, the topic is approached in a different style, chosen so that students will be able to experience a variety of genres such as newspaper and magazine articles, interviews, pamphlets, charts, and advertisements. Photographs occasionally serve as prompts to assist comprehension, or to stimulate curiosity and conversation about the topics.

Reading Comprehension

The reading comprehension section is composed of three sections.

• **Check Your Predictions**—Students are asked to evaluate their predicting ability.

• **Check the Facts**—Students answer factual questions. This is meant to be fairly simple and the exercise can be completed individually or in groups.

• **Analyze**—This section will include more sophisticated questions that will have students make inferences, as well as analyze and synthesize the information they have read.

Vocabulary Work

Vocabulary Work has two sections.

• **Guess Meaning from Context**—Exercises highlight probable unknown vocabulary words that students should be able to guess using different types of contextual clues. Some of the most common clues students should be looking for include: internal definitions, *restatement* or synonyms that precede or follow the new word, and examples. However, one of the most powerful ways to guess is to use *real world* knowledge. Students must learn to trust their own ability to make educated guesses about meaning based on their own experience. Matching vocabulary exercises are found in the back of the student book.

• **Guess Meaning from Related Words**—This section focuses on words that can be guessed through morphological analysis. Although morphology is a "context clue," it is so important, that it requires a chapter section of its own. The more students learn to recognize related words, the faster their vocabularies will grow. Students who speak languages such as Spanish—a language that has a large number of cognates or words that look similar to their English counterparts—should also be encouraged to use their native language knowledge as well.

Reading Skills

This section focuses on helpful reading skills and strategies, such as identifying cohesive elements, analyzing organization, understanding tone, and detecting bias.

Discussion

Questions in this section are designed to encourage class or group discussion. For instructors wishing to follow-up the readings with writing responses, it would be helpful for students to first discuss and then write their individual opinions and/or summarize those of their peers.

PART II

Readings in Part II have been written to be more challenging than those in Part I, so students are asked to read only for the most important ideas. The readings are written so that

• important ideas are stated more than once.
• important ideas are not obscured by difficult vocabulary and high-level structures.
• vocabulary from Part I readings is "built in" or recycled.
• some "new" vocabulary words are forms of words already seen in Part I.

Two activity sections follow the Part II reading. The first consists of questions that will help

students pinpoint the main ideas. The second asks students to make educated guesses about vocabulary they encountered in Part I.

Idea Exchange

Each chapter ends with a comprehensive discussion activity called Idea Exchange. This activity has two steps.

• **Think about Your Ideas**—This section is a structured exercise that helps students clarify their thoughts before they are asked to speak. By filling out charts, answering questions, or putting items in order, students clarify their ideas on the topic.

• **Talk about Your Ideas**—The language in this activity is directly applicable to the discussion questions in the step above.

CNN Video Activities

The CNN video news clip activities at the back of the student text are thematically related to each chapter. Activities are designed to recycle themes and vocabulary from each chapter, and to encourage further class discussion and written responses.

A Word on Methodology and Classroom Management

Class Work, Group Work, Pair Work, and Individual Work

One of the most basic questions a teacher must decide before beginning an activity is whether it is best done as class work, group work, or individual work. Each has its place in the language classroom. For some activities, the answer is obvious. Reading should always be an individual activity. Reading aloud to the class can be pronunciation practice for the reader or listening practice for the listeners, but it is not reading for comprehension.

On the other hand, many activities in this text can be done successfully in pairs, groups, or with the entire class working together. If possible, a mix of individual, pair, group, and class work is probably best. For example, two students may work together and then share their work with a larger group that then shares its ideas with the entire class.

Some rules of thumb are:

• Pair work is often most successful in activities that have one right answer. Pairs should be able to check their answers or at least share them with the class.

• Groups work best when one group member records the discussion, so that the group can then report to the class. In this way, everyone gets the maximum benefit.

• Think of yourself as the manager of a whole class activity rather than the focal point. Make sure that students talk to each other, not just to you. For example, you might appoint yourself secretary and write students' ideas on the board as they are talking.

Error Correction

Language errors are bound to occur in discussions at this level. However, the purpose of the discussions in this text is fluency not accuracy. Therefore, errors should not be dealt with unless they make comprehension difficult or impossible. Make unobtrusive notes about persistent errors that you want to deal with later. In those cases where it is difficult to understand what a student is trying to say, first give the student a chance to clarify. If they cannot do this, restate what you think they are trying to say.

Dictionaries

Frequent dictionary use makes reading a slow, laborious affair. Students should be taught first to try to guess the meaning of a word using context and word form clues before they resort to a dictionary. In addition, although a good learner's English-English dictionary is helpful, bilingual dictionaries should be discouraged, as they are often inaccurate. Students should use a dictionary that supplies simple and clear definitions, context sentences, and synonyms. We recommend *Heinle's Newbury House Dictionary with CD-ROM, 3rd Edition.*

Finally, thanks to all instructors who, by selecting the *Hot Topics* series, recognize that ESL students are mature learners who have the right to read about unconventional and provocative topics. By offering your students challenging reading topics that encourage curiosity and debate, their ideas and opinions will become essential and fruitful parts of their classroom experience.

CHERYL PAVLIK

ACKNOWLEDGMENTS

As is always the case, this text has been molded by many minds. My sincere thanks to James Brown for believing in the project from the start, then ably defending my ideas to others, while just as eloquently explaining their concerns to me. Thanks to Sherrise Roehr for her enthusiasm and advocacy of this project. I also owe a great debt to Sarah Barnicle, an editor and a friend, who shared my joy at the triumph of the Red Sox and my disappointment as world events didn't unfold the way we'd so hoped. She was a true editorial trifecta—infinitely patient, resolutely upbeat, and unfailingly diplomatic. And to Maryellen Eschmann-Killeen and Tunde Dewey for making certain my ideas became a book.

We also would like to thank the following reviewers:

Chiou-Lan Chern
National Taiwan Normal University, Taipei, Taiwan

C.J. Dalton
Institution Verbatim English, Belo Horizante, Brazil

Judith Finkelstein
Reseda Community Adult School, Reseda, CA, United States

Patricia Brenner
University of Washington, Seattle, WA, United States

Renee Klosz
Lindsey Hopkins Technical Education Center, Miami, FL, United States

Eric Rosenbaum
BEGIN Managed Programs, New York, NY, United States

CHAPTER

REALITY TV: WOULD YOU BE A SURVIVOR?

PREVIEW

Discuss the answers to these questions.

1. Check the columns.

Which type of program . . .	Reality TV	News	TV Comedy or Drama
is entertainment?			
uses actors?			
has a script that is written before the program?			
gives important information?			
is often surprising or embarrassing?			
offers people money or valuable opportunities?			
claims that it shows how people react in real situations?			

2. Is reality television popular in your country? If so, which programs are the most popular?

PART I

Predict

A. Scan the reading and make predictions.

1. How many reality programs are discussed?

   a. 2   b. 3   c. 4

2. Which program began in the Netherlands?

   a. *Survivor*

   b. *Temptation Island*

   c. *Big Brother*

3. Which program gives away $1,000,000?

   a. *Survivor*

   b. *Fear Factor*

   c. *Big Brother*

B. Skim the reading to answer these questions.

4. Why did the writer choose to talk about these programs?

   a. Because they are good reality TV programs.

   b. Because they are popular reality programs.

   c. Because they are unusual reality programs.

5. What is the writer's purpose?

   a. To describe the programs.

   b. To encourage people to watch the programs.

   c. To judge the programs.

C. What do you want to know? Write at least two questions about the article.

_____

_____

Read It

Read the article. Look for the answers to your questions from Exercise C on page 2.

 (READING)   A Guide to Reality TV

1   Reality television programs are growing in popularity. There are many different types, but all of them have one thing in common—they make ordinary people famous, if only for a few days. Here is a sample of some of the most popular shows.

Big Brother

5   This popular program originated in the Netherlands. Many different countries have adapted the program. On *Big Brother*, ten people live in a house together. The housemates cannot contact the outside

10   world. There is no TV, radio, telephone, the Internet, newspapers, or any other forms of media. The contestants have to share the housework. In addition, "Big

Brother" gives them a special job or task every week. These tasks test their

15   ability to work as a team. In most countries, the audience votes to eliminate one of the competitors each week. In the United States, however, the contestants vote, but the public doesn't.

Fear Factor

On this program, contestants "face their fears" to win money. In order to win, they have to do

20   many things to test their courage. For example, they often have to eat live worms and other small animals such as insects. In addition, their bodies may be covered with bees or they may be asked to get inside a box full of snakes. There

25   are many different types of *Fear Factor* teams. Some of the teams consist of female competitors; other teams are made up of siblings. There have even been parent and child teams. The producers of *Fear Factor* say that all the stunts have been tested. Indeed, no one has been injured yet.

Survivor

30 One very popular reality show is
Survivor. On this program, 16
people compete for $1,000,000.
They must live outside and cook
their own food. They often have to

35 catch it as well. In addition, the
competitors must perform
different kinds of physical tests.
Every week the competitors vote
out one member of their group.

40 The producers say that the competition depends on the competitors'
ability to survive in the wilderness. However, understanding politics is
actually the most important skill. Successful players must be able to
make agreements with other players. If they cannot do this, the other
competitors will eliminate them. When only two people are left, the

45 previously eliminated contestants vote to give one of the finalists
$1,000,000.

Temptation Island

Temptation Island takes four couples to a
tropical island. The couples are not
married, but they have serious

50 relationships. On the island, the
couples are separated. The four
women stay with 13 handsome
bachelors. The four men stay with a
group of beautiful single women. The

55 single men and women are supposed
to tempt the members of each couple
to leave their mates. If a single person
can convince a man or woman to leave his or her mate, he or she wins.
Many religious organizations are upset about this show. They say that it is

60 immoral because it is about sex, not relationships. A television executive
defends the show. He says that it helps couples learn about themselves.

Reading Comprehension

Check Your Predictions

1. Look back at questions 1–5 in the Predict sections A and B. How accurate was your skimming and scanning?

Prediction	Not Accurate	Accurate
1		
2		
3		
4		
5		

2. Did you find the answers to your questions from Exercise C? What were they?

_____

_____

Check the Facts

Check (✓) the questions you can answer after one reading. Then go back and look for the answers that you are unsure of.

_____ 1. How many people live together on *Big Brother?*

_____ 2. How much contact can people on *Big Brother* have with the outside world?

_____ 3. Who votes people out of the house in *Big Brother* in the United States?

_____ 4. Name one thing that people on *Fear Factor* have to do.

_____ 5. What are some different kinds of *Fear Factor* teams?

_____ 6. How do the contestants on *Survivor* live?

_____ 7. What do successful survivors have to be able to do?

_____ 8. Who votes to give the final survivor $1,000,000?

_____ 9. How many couples go to *Temptation Island?*

_____ 10. How does a single person win the game on *Temptation Island?*

_____ 11. Why do some people criticize the show?

_____ 12. How did a television executive defend the program?

Analyze

1. How are *Survivor* and *Big Brother* similar to each other? How are they different?
2. Which of the four reality programs is the most different from the others?
3. Which program do you think would be the most fun? The most difficult?

Vocabulary Work

Guess Meaning from Context

1. Work with a partner. Look back at the reading and try to guess the meaning of these words.

Word	Line	Meaning
media	12	_____
worms	21	_____
relationships	50, 60	_____
separated	51	_____
convince	58	_____

2. Then turn to page 163 and match the actual meanings with the words.
3. Look at the words you guessed correctly. Look back at the reading. What clues did you use to understand the meaning?

Guess Meaning from Related Words

1. These words contain words that you may know. Underline the familiar words. Then guess the meaning of the whole word.

reality	_____
contestant	_____
wilderness	_____
agreement	_____
housework	_____
housemate	_____

2. Find a related word(s) in the reading.

compete _____ _____

survivor _____

tempt _____

Reading Skills

Understanding Cohesion

Writers often use different words to refer to the same things. Find other words that mean the same thing.

players _____ _____

audience _____

task _____

program _____

Discussion

1. Describe another reality TV show you have seen.

2. Would you like to be on a reality television show? Which one would you choose? Why?

PART II

This reading is more difficult than the article in Part I. Read it for the main ideas. Do not worry if you cannot understand everything.

Read It

Read to find the answers to these questions.

1. What are two reasons why people think that reality TV is popular?

2. According to the scientific study, what kind of people enjoy reality TV?

What's So Great about Reality TV?

1 Even if you do not watch reality television, you can probably name some of the programs. Your friends and co-workers talk about them. You read about the shows in the newspapers, see pictures in magazines, and even see contestants on the news.

5 Why are these shows so popular? Some people say that people watch the programs to be part of the "in" crowd. Other people think that only people who are unintelligent watch reality television.

Steven Reiss and James Wiltz are psychologists at Ohio State University. They wanted to find out what kind of people watch reality 10 programs and why, so they conducted a scientific study. The results were surprising. First of all, they discovered that reality television watchers are not less intelligent than non-watchers. They also found out that they are not more social than non-watchers, so they do not watch these programs just to talk about them with friends.

15 They did find that people who watch reality television were more competitive than people who don't watch it. However, that was not the biggest difference. The attitude that separated watchers from non-watchers was the importance of social status. People who enjoy reality television generally agreed with statements such as "Prestige is important to me" and 20 "I am impressed with designer clothes." The desire for status is a way to get attention. When you get more attention, you feel more important.

Through reality TV, people can dream about becoming famous. Ordinary people watch other ordinary people become celebrities. The message of reality television is that ordinary people can become so 25 important that millions will watch them. And the secret dream of many of those viewers is that they might be the next celebrities.

Vocabulary Work

Guess Meaning from Related Words

Find new forms of these words from Part II.

	New Word	Meaning
compete	_____	_____
celebrate	_____	_____
intelligent	_____	_____

Idea Exchange

Think about Your Ideas

Choose <u>one</u> sentence from A and <u>one</u> sentence from B. Then complete the sentences so that they are true for you.

A. I never watch reality TV because _____.

   I watch reality TV shows that are _____.

   I enjoy reality TV shows because _____.

B. I would like to be on a reality TV show because _____.

   I might be on a reality TV show if _____.

   I would never be on a reality TV show because _____.

Talk about Your Ideas

1. Do you watch reality TV shows? Why or why not?
2. Would you like to be on a reality TV show? Why or why not?

For CNN video activities about reality TV, turn to page 168.

CHAPTER ❷

Violence in Sports:
When is a game
not a game?

PREVIEW

1. Read the interviews.

From the Street

Reporter: Riots after sports events are in the news more and more these days. In your opinion, what is causing this violence?

Joey G.: My friends and I go to football games all the time. When a team wins a big game, the fans want to be crazy and have a good time. That's normal. There just should be more police.

Ellen: I don't go to soccer matches anymore. I worry about alcohol at the games. That's the problem. When people drink, they do stupid things.

Julie: The troublemakers aren't real fans. They just want to be in a big crowd and act crazy. They shouldn't allow those people to go to the games.

Herman: Fans get angry if their team loses—especially if it's a big game. They should keep the two groups of fans apart. That's the cause of the problem.

2. Do you agree with any of the comments? Why or why not?

PART I

Predict

Skim the three readings and make predictions.

1. Look at the titles and the format.

    a. Are the readings from a textbook? Explain why or why not.

    b. Are the readings from a newspaper? Explain why or why not.

2. Guess which article will answer each question. Write the number of the article in the space.

    a. What happened after a football game?
    Reading _____

    b. Why were there riots in Moscow?
    Reading _____

    c. What's happening in Japan next week?
    Reading _____

3. In your opinion, which two articles are the most similar? Why do you think so?

4. What do you want to know? Write one question for each article.

    _____

    _____

    _____

    _____

    _____

    _____

Read It

Read the articles. Scan for the answers to your questions.

READING 1

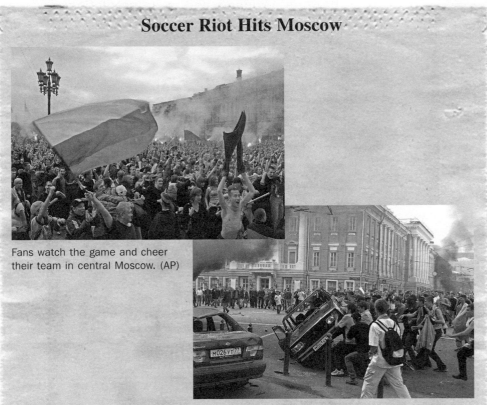

Soccer Riot Hits Moscow

Fans watch the game and cheer their team in central Moscow. (AP)

Fans became angry and started overturning cars.

MOSCOW—Officials said about 50 people were injured and two died in a riot after Japan beat Russia 1–0. Police said about 8,000 fans took part in the riot. They arrested 60. Thousands of fans watched the game on a large outdoor screen. When Russia lost, the riot started.

Fans rioted, burning cars and smashing store windows. Thousands ran through the streets shouting "Forward, Russia!" and other soccer slogans. One reporter said, "It looked like a war zone." One Moscow official said, "We will not show matches on outdoor screens again. That was a big mistake."

Victory Celebration Turns Ugly

COLUMBUS—Police arrested 46 people in a celebratory riot after Ohio State University's football team defeated the University of Michigan 14–9. At first, the students were celebrating in the streets. Then, at about midnight, a mob of students started a fire and began burning furniture. Meanwhile, another group began overturning cars and setting them on fire. They destroyed nine cars before police arrived. Police used pepper spray and wooden bullets against the crowd. The rioters threw bottles and cans at the police. "They can't stop it," said one student. "We're the best. No one can stop us!" Police had control of most areas by 4:15 A.M.

After this violent celebration, university officials said that they would punish the rioters. "I'd like to say most of these people are not our students, but unfortunately they *are* our students," said Bill Hall, vice president of student affairs at Ohio State. "We will watch the videos and find the students. They will have to leave the university."

World Cup Worries

TOKYO—The World Cup finals begin in Japan next Friday. People here are both excited and worried. They're excited about the games and worried about the fans. Japan is no stranger to international competition. The Olympics were here 1964, 1972, and 1998. But soccer fans are very different from Olympic fans.

Riots and fights never happen at the Olympics. However, they are common after soccer games. In 1985, 39 Italian fans died in a mob riot after the European Cup Final between Liverpool of England and Juventus of Italy turned ugly.

As a result, the Japanese are particularly worried about the fans from England. The British government thinks that between 6,000 and 8,000 British fans will attend the World Cup. Officials want to make sure that there are no problems, such as property destruction. Therefore, last Friday, England banned more than 1,000 possible troublemakers from traveling to Japan. "Ninety-nine percent of our fans are not interested in violence. The other one percent will not be allowed to come," said Kevin Miles of the Football Supporters' Association.

However, Japanese citizens are making their own plans. Many parents will not let their children go to the games. Businesses near the stadium will not open on the days of the matches. Perhaps these people know the song that the Chelsea Shedboys sing at their team's games:

> We're forever throwing bottles
> Pretty bottles in the air.
> They fly so high
> They nearly touch the sky.
> And like West Ham* they
>   fade and die.
> Arsenal* keep running;
>   Wolves and Tottenham* too.
> We're the Chelsea Shedboys;
> We'll keep running after you!

*West Ham, Arsenal, Wolves and Tottenham are soccer teams

Reading Comprehension

Check Your Predictions

1. How good were your predictions in the Predict section on page 11?

Prediction	Not Accurate	Accurate
1		
2		
3		

2. If you found the answers to your questions in Predict #4, what were they?

_____

_____

_____

Check the Facts

Read the statements and write *true* (T) or *false* (F). Go back to the readings and look for the answers you are unsure of.

READING 1

_____ 1. Russia defeated Japan 1–0.

_____ 2. Thousands of people watched the game outside.

_____ 3. The police arrested 60 people.

_____ 4. Two people died.

_____ 5. The rioters smashed windows in the Kremlin.

READING 2

_____ 1. Students were angry because their team lost the game.

_____ 2. The rioters burned cars.

_____ 3. Almost 50 people died in the riots.

_____ 4. Most of the rioters were not students.

_____ 5. The university isn't going to punish the troublemakers.

_____ 1. People in Japan like soccer.

_____ 2. Japanese soccer fans are often violent.

_____ 3. About 80,000 English fans will attend the World Cup finals.

_____ 4. Some English soccer fans will not be able to travel to Japan.

_____ 5. Very few English soccer fans are troublemakers.

Analyze

1. How were the riots in Russia similar to the riots after the university football game? How were they different?

2. What do the Russian officials think was the cause of the riot in Moscow?

3. How are the Olympics similar to World Cup soccer games? How are they different?

4. Are the Chelsea Shedboys troublemakers? Why or why not?

Vocabulary Work

Guess Meaning from Context

1. Read the score and write *true* (T) or *false* (F).

New York Yankees 6   Los Angeles Dodgers 4

_____ a. The Dodgers won the game.

_____ b. The Yankees didn't lose the game.

_____ c. The Yankees defeated the Dodgers.

_____ d. The Dodgers beat the Yankees.

2. Work with a partner. Look back at the readings and try to guess the meaning of these words.

Word	Reading	Meaning
fan	1	_____
arrest	1 & 2	_____
riot	1 & 2 & 3	_____
injured	1	_____
mob	2 & 3	_____
smash	1	_____
shout	1	_____
ban	3	_____

3. Turn to page 163 and check the actual meanings with your guesses.

4. Look at the words you guessed correctly. Look back at the readings. What clues did you use?

Guess Meaning from Related Words

You can sometimes guess the meaning of new words by relating them to words you know. For example: We always <u>win</u> the championship. We are the <u>winners</u>.

1. Scan the readings for other forms of the words below.

Verb	Noun (thing)	Noun (person)	Adjective
	riot		—
—	violence	—	
		celebrity	
	destruction	—	—

2. Some words are made up of two common words. Write the two words on the lines.

   troublemaker (n) _____ _____

   overturn (v) _____ _____

3. Look at these phrases. Can you guess their meanings?

   a war zone _____

   turned ugly _____

Reading Skills

Understanding Organization

1. News articles have a special organization. A summary of the news story appears at the beginning of the article. Look back at the three readings and underline each summary.

2. Which news article is:

   a. an explanation?   b. in time order?   c. a description?

   Underline sentences or phrases that support your answers.

Discussion

1. Are there riots at sports events in your country? Why or why not?

2. Have you ever seen sports violence? What happened?

PART II

This reading is more difficult than the articles in Part I. Read it for the main ideas. Do not worry if you cannot understand everything.

Read It

Read to find the answers to these questions.

1. What are the two main causes of mob violence?
2. How can officials stop violence at sports events?

 READING

Psychologists Study the Causes of Mob Violence

What is the connection between violence and sports? Psychologists say that there are many reasons for violence at sports events. One is alcohol. Many fans drink a lot at games. When people drink, they are more likely to do abnormal things. Psychologist Dennis Brock says, "Quiet people become loud. Normally nonviolent people become destructive."

David Sampson, a sports sociologist, agrees. "These are often celebratory riots—a large number of very happy people mixed in with large amounts of alcohol. They don't often seem dangerous in the beginning, but things get violent quickly."

Another reason for violence at sports events is the crowd itself. When individuals are in a large group of people, they can lose their sense of personal responsibility. Edward Hirt, a social psychologist, says that research shows that people do things in crowds that they would never do alone. People in crowds feel anonymous—no one knows who they are. Crowds also make people feel powerful. They stop making personal decisions. They just follow the crowd. Social psychologists call this a "mob mentality."

Dave Zarifis, head of public safety at Northern Iowa University says, "Some people don't even come to celebrate. They want to drink hard and make trouble. Someone does something stupid, and it grows from there. You get a mob mentality. People think it's OK to do almost anything. They think, 'There are so many of us and not enough of them.'"

Social psychologist Dr. Sharon Kennedy says that there are a few things officials can do to prevent violence. Making sure that an area is not overcrowded is very important. Officials should also think of games as "big parties." Then they will prepare differently. Kennedy says that in Great Britain they are controlling the problem with cameras in all the stadiums. "When you know someone is watching, you are much less likely to behave badly."

Vocabulary Work

Guess Meaning from Related Words

Find other forms of these words. Write the words you found in the reading. Write what you think each word means.

	Word	Other Form(s)		Meaning
1.	destroy	_____		_____
2.	celebrate	_____		_____
3.	normal	_____	_____	_____
4.	violent	_____		_____
5.	crowd	_____		_____

Idea Exchange

Think about Your Ideas

1. Check the correct columns.

People at the sports events . . .	usually	often	sometimes	rarely	never
drink alcohol.					
get drunk.					
start fights.					
use bad language.					
throw things.					
destroy property.					
other					

2. Number the solutions to the problem of sports violence from most (1) to least (8) effective. Add your own solution to the list.

_____ place cameras in the stadiums

_____ enforce crowd control

_____ increase ticket prices

_____ place more police in the stadiums

_____ prohibit alcohol in the stadiums

_____ prohibit alcohol in the parking lot

_____ prohibit fans from watching the game on screens outside the stadiums

_____ search every fan for weapons

_____ other _____

Talk about Your Ideas

1. How do people behave at sports events you go to? Are you ever worried about violence?

2. What should authorities do about fan violence? Explain what will work and what won't work.

For CNN video activities about violence at sporting events,
turn to page 169.

CHAPTER ③

ADVERTISING:
WE KNOW WHAT YOU WANT *BEFORE* YOU DO!

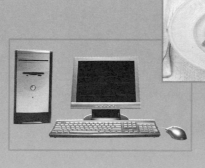

PREVIEW

1. How do you decide what items to buy? Complete the chart.

	Advertising	Friends	Popularity	Price	Other
clothes					
electronics (computer, stereo, etc.)					
car					
food					
restaurant					

2. Think of two or three things that you would like to buy right now. (It doesn't matter if you can afford them or not.) How do you find out about each one? Why do you want each one?

PART I

Predict

Skim the three readings and make predictions. Which article or articles . . .

1. came from a newspaper? How do you know?
2. will discuss advertising awards?
3. will probably criticize advertising?
4. will discuss a new kind of advertising technique?
5. Write a question that you think each article may answer.

_____

_____

_____

Read It

As you read the articles, look for the answers to the questions in the Predict section.

 READING 1

Will Anyone Notice the Shoes?

NEW YORK—In 1997 the Candie's shoe company introduced an ad that was very controversial. Some people thought it was funny. Other people thought it was in bad taste. The ad was a picture of Jenny McCarthy, a TV star, sitting on a toilet wearing Candie's shoes. Then in 2003 the company created another bathroom ad. This time they put "American Idol" winner Kelly Clarkson in the bathtub. Although some people thought the ads were offensive, they were effective. In fact, they worked so well that, in 2004, the company put the two ads together. Neil Cole, chief executive officer of Candie's Inc., explains why they chose these ads. "It is difficult to be noticed in advertising," he said, "Our customers expect us to be creative. They also expect us to use famous people like Jenny McCarthy and Kelly Clarkson. They remember the ads and our company and that's good for us."

 READING 2   And the Winner Is . . .

Buy Cover Girl makeup. (You will be beautiful.) Wear Nike sneakers. (You will be strong.) Drive a Lexus. (You will be successful.) Drink Budweiser. (You will be popular.) Advertising's promises can seem harmless, but a group of critics, scholars, and journalists argue that they aren't. They have formed a group called the Media and Democracy Congress. This group wants to teach Americans how influential advertising can be. In order to do this, they give advertisers

awards for bad ads. The name of these awards, the Schmios, rhyme with the Clios—the Oscars of the advertising industry. Every advertising agency would like to win a Clio. No one wants a Schmio.

Schmios are given for false advertising and for some ads that are just in bad taste. For example, TV star Jenny McCarthy won a Schmio a few years ago for an ad that pictures her sitting on the toilet and reading the *Wall Street Journal*. The National Rifle Association also won an award for its Eddie Eagle ads. Eddie is cute and cuddly and loves to teach kids about guns. He tells children, "If you see a gun, STOP! Don't touch. Leave the area. Tell an adult." But critics think the NRA is sending another message. "We gave Eddie Eagle a special award for the most effective contribution to our culture of violence," said Bianca Jagger, a Schmio presenter.

Shoe company Nike was given a "Lifetime Achievement" award. Charles Kernaghan, executive director of the National Labor Committee, presented the award to the company that spends about $640 million a year on advertising around the world. He pointed out that many of Nike's ads show the empowerment of women. However, critics argue that Nike doesn't empower its workers—particularly women. In fact, it treats them very badly. Their salaries are low and their working conditions are terrible.

Peter Zapf, an advertising expert and a member of the Clio board, defends the Clios. "We honor advertising excellence," but not even he can completely defend his industry. "Most advertising is bad," admits Zapf. "Very few advertising companies respect the customers' intelligence."

 **READING 3**   Undercover Marketing

You're in a department store and you see a couple of attractive young women looking at a sweater. You listen to their conversation

"I can't believe it—a Lorenzo Bertolla! They're almost impossible to find. Isn't it beautiful? And it's a lot cheaper than the one Sara bought in Rome."

They leave and you go over to see this *incredible* sweater. It's nice and the price is right. You've never heard of Lorenzo Bertolla, but those girls looked really stylish. They *must* know. So, you buy it. You never realize that those young women are employees of an advertising agency. They are actually paid to go from store to store, talking loudly about Lorenzo Bertolla clothes.

Every day we notice what people are wearing, driving, and eating. If the person looks cool, the product seems cool, too. This is the secret of undercover marketing. Companies from Ford to Nike are starting to use it.

Undercover marketing is important because it reaches people that don't pay attention to traditional advertising. This is particularly true of the MTV generation—consumers between the ages of 18 and 34. It is a golden group. They have a lot of money to spend, but they don't trust ads.

So advertising agencies hire young actors to "perform" in bars and other places where young adults go. Some people might call this practice deceptive, but marketing executive Jonathan Ressler calls it creative. "Look at traditional advertising. Its effectiveness is decreasing."

John Palumbo, another industry expert, is sure that underground marketing is the right way to reach young people. "A product has to have credibility to succeed," he says. "People have to see it. They have to understand it in a real way. The best way to do that is to put it in their world. And that's what we do. We put the product in their life."

However, one might ask what exactly is "real" about two young women pretending to be enthusiastic about a sweater? Advertising executives would say it's no less real than an ad. The difference is that you know an ad is trying to persuade you to buy something. You don't know when a conversation you overhear is just a performance.

Reading Comprehension

Check Your Predictions

1. How good were your predictions on page 22?

Prediction	Not Accurate	Accurate
1		
2		
3		
4		

2. If you found the answers to your questions in the Predict section, what were they?

_____

_____

_____

Check the Facts

Mark the statements *true* (T) or *false* (F). Then go back to the readings and look for the answers you are unsure of.

(**READING 1**)

_____ 1. Candies are shoes.

_____ 2. Jenny McCarthy and Kelly Clarkson are models.

_____ 3. The bathroom ads made people buy more shoes.

_____ 4. Young people didn't like these ads.

READING 2

_____ 1. The Media and Democracy Congress gives awards for good advertising.

_____ 2. Advertisers want to win Schmios.

_____ 3. The Candie's™ shoe ad won a Clio™.

_____ 4. The Eddie Eagle ads won a Schmio.

_____ 5. Nike™ got a special award for helping its workers.

READING 3

_____ 1. Young people often don't trust advertisements.

_____ 2. Undercover marketing uses models to advertise products.

_____ 3. Undercover marketing works because everyone wants quality products.

_____ 4. The MTV generation is over 50.

_____ 5. Undercover marketing is done in schools and universities.

Analyze

1. How is the advertising technique in Reading 1 similar to the advertising technique in Reading 3?

2. How do you think the Media and Democracy Congress feels about undercover marketing? Why?

Vocabulary Work

Guess Meaning from Context

1. Work with a partner. Look back at the readings and try to guess the meanings of these words and phrases.

Word/Phrase	Reading	Meaning
controversial	1	_____
in bad taste	1	_____
awards	2	_____
false	2	_____
cool	3	_____
deceptive	3	_____
enthusiastic	3	_____

2. Turn to page 163 and match the actual meanings with the words.

3. Look at the words you guessed correctly. Look back at the reading. What clues did you use?

4. Sometimes we can ignore an unknown word in a series of words if we understand the other words in the list. Does it matter if you know exactly what *scholars* are in the sentence below?

    Advertising's promises can seem harmless, but a group of critics, <u>scholars,</u> and journalists argue that they aren't.

    This is often true for adjectives. It is often enough to know if the adjective is a positive or negative quality. Is *cuddly* positive or negative in the sentence below?

    Eddie is cute and <u>cuddly</u> and loves to teach kids about guns.

5. Sometimes grammar helps us guess whether an adjective is positive or negative. One of the adjectives below is positive and one is negative. How do we know which one is positive?

    Although some people thought the ads were <u>offensive</u>, they were <u>effective</u>.

Guess Meaning from Related Words

1. Use the individual parts of these words to guess their meanings.

READING 2

Word	Meaning
harmless	_____
influential	_____
critics	_____
empowerment	_____
empower	_____

Word	Meaning
undercover	_____
stylish	_____
traditional	_____
underground	_____
overhear	_____
performance	_____

2. Sometimes writers use familiar words in a slightly different way from their normal usage. Look at the underlined word. Is it usually a noun or a verb? What is it in the phrase below?

an ad that <u>pictures</u> her

3. Look at the underlined word. What does it usually mean? What does it mean here?

It is a <u>golden</u> group.

Reading Skills

Identifying Cultural References

1. Look at these cultural references. What do they have in common? Which ones can be grouped together?

Wall Street Journal   *American Idol*   the Oscars

The MTV generation   National Labor Committee   Ford

Nike   Lexus   Cover Girl   National Rifle Association

2. Is it important to know exactly what these references are? Why or why not?

Understanding Cohesion

Who is *they* in each sentence? Write your answers below.

This time <u>they</u> put *American Idol* winner Kelly Clarkson in the bathtub.
      1

Although some people thought the ads were offensive, <u>they</u> were effective.
                                                      2

In fact, <u>they</u> worked so well that, in 2004, the company put the two ads
         3

together. Neil Cole, chief executive officer of Candie's Inc., explains why

<u>they</u> chose these ads, ". . . Our customers expect us to be creative. <u>They</u> also
 4   5

expect us to use famous people like Jenny McCarthy and Kelly Clarkson.

<u>They</u> remember the ads and our company and that's good for us."
 6

1. _____

2. _____

3. _____

4. _____

5. _____

6. _____

Discussion

1. Do you think that undercover marketing is worse than traditional advertising? Why or why not?

2. Do you think that advertising is harmful or helpful to consumers? Why?

PART II

This reading is more difficult than the articles in Part I. Read it for the main ideas. Do not worry if you cannot understand everything.

Read It

Read to find the answers to these questions.

Which strategy

1. tries to make you feel good?

2. uses negative advertising?

3. uses famous people?

 READING   Advertising Strategies

Advertisers have many methods to get you to try a product and be loyal to it. Lots of times, what they are selling is a lifestyle, or an image, rather than the product. Here are some ways they get us to spend money on things we may not want.

Ideal Families—always seem perfect. The kids are cool and they have the hottest fashions, haircuts, and toys. Ideal families are all attractive—and they never argue! Ideal families represent the types of people that people watching the ad would like to be.

Family Fun—an ad that shows a product bringing families together or helping them have fun together. For example, Mom or Dad brings home the "right" food and a boring dinner turns into a family party.

Excitement—Food is great fun! One bite of this and you're surfing in California or soaring on your skateboard!

Star Power—Your favorite sports star or celebrity is telling you that this product is the best! It's very effective. People listen and they usually don't remember that the star is paid to support the product.

Bandwagon—Join the in-crowd! Don't be left out! Everyone is buying this—Why aren't you?

Put Downs—Advertisers criticize the competitor's product to make their own product seem better.

Facts and Figures—Advertisers use facts and statistics to make their statements more credible. Unfortunately these "facts" are often not completely true.

Repetition—Advertisers hope that if you see a product or hear its name over and over again, you will be more likely to buy it. Sometimes the same commercial will be repeated over and over again during the same television program.

Heart Strings—Ads tell you a story that make you feel good. For example, one McDonalds commercial shows a dad and his son shoveling snow together. When they finish, the son buys his dad lunch at McDonalds.

Sounds Good—Music and other sound effects add to the excitement of commercials. Those little tunes that you just can't get out of your head make you think of the product. Have you ever noticed that the commercials are louder than the program?

Cartoon Characters—Tony the Tiger sells cereal and the Nestlés Nesquik Bunny sells chocolate milk. Cartoons like these help kids identify with products.

Misleading Words—Advertisers are supposed to tell the truth, but sometimes they use words that can mislead viewers. Look for phrases in commercials like *part of, the taste of real, natural, new, better tasting,* and *because we care.* There are hundreds of these deceptive phrases.

Omission—Advertisers don't give you the entire story about their product. For example, an ad claims that a sugary cereal is *part* of a healthy breakfast. It doesn't claim that the breakfast is healthy (or even healthier) without this product.

Are You Cool Enough?—Advertisers try to convince you that if you don't use their products, you are not cool. Usually advertisers do this by showing people who look uncool trying a product and then suddenly becoming hip.

Vocabulary Work

Guess the meaning of these words. What clues did you use?

1. strategies _____
2. lifestyle _____
3. hottest _____
4. in-crowd _____
5. left out _____
6. competitor _____
7. statistics _____
8. misleading _____
9. deceptive _____
10. sugary _____
11. uncool _____
12. hip _____

Reading Skills

Understanding the Author's Viewpoint

1. What is the writer's opinion of advertising?

   _____

   _____

2. Find at least three things the writer says that support your answer.

   _____

   _____

   _____

Idea Exchange

Think about Your Ideas

1. Write the names of product brands that you always buy. Then write what you like about each one.

   Brand   What You Like about It

   _____   _____

   _____   _____

   _____   _____

2. How loyal are you to this brand?

   Do you buy it even if a similar brand is much cheaper?

   If the store doesn't have your brand, do you wait and buy it somewhere else?

3. How much do you identify with this product or brand?

   Do your friends know that you only use this brand?

   Would you feel bad if the company changed this product, or would you just buy something else?

Talk about Your Ideas

Do you agree or disagree with this statement?

A brand is like the product's personality. It's how consumers feel about it. It's the affection they feel for it—the trust and loyalty they give it. Above all, it's the shared experience they have with it. For example, Dove Beauty Bar (soap) has grown into a worldwide brand because of its relationship with women. Hershey's Kisses, Guinness Stout, and Pepsi all mean much more to their users than chocolate, beer, and soda—from www.ogilvy.com

For CNN video activities about advertising, turn to page 170.

For CNN video activities about advertising, turn to page 170.

CHAPTER 4

FASHION: You mean you're wearing *THAT?*

PREVIEW

Discuss the answers to these questions.

1. Look at these pictures. What can you tell about the people from the clothing that they are wearing?

2. Do any of these clothes seem unusual to you? If so, why?

PART I

Predict

Skim the three readings and make predictions.

1. Which of these articles are probably from a newspaper?
2. Which article will . . .
   - talk about men's clothing in history?
   - discuss high school students?
   - talk about work clothes?
3. Which articles mention specific kinds of clothing?
4. Write a question that you think each article may answer.

_____

_____

_____

Read It

Read the articles. Look for the answers to your questions.

 READING 1   Designed to Fit In

Go to the mall and look at the young teenagers. Many of them are wearing the same clothes. As an adult, you might think, "Why do they want to look identical?"

"Wearing the *right* clothes is very important for young teenagers, especially girls," says Kathleen Jackson from Delmar Hunt School in Lincoln, Nebraska. "Looking right means fitting in."

"It's a sign of normal child development," Mrs. Jackson says. "Young teenagers are starting to separate from their parents, and they want to fit in with their friends. Dressing alike is one way to do that."

Dr. Adam Robb, a psychiatrist at Emory University, calls this *peer group identity.* Before forming their own identity, teenagers become part of a group to feel accepted and secure. He says, "Teenagers judge each other all the time. In many schools, one of the ways you fit in is to look like everyone else—you wear the *right* skirt or pants or carry the *right* backpack."

Fashion can be a lot of fun, but it has another side, too. Sometimes the pressure of dressing in a certain way creates problems, especially in families with no money for expensive clothes. Some schools have found a solution to this problem. They have a dress code or make students wear uniforms. "Students were laughed at if they didn't have the right clothes. That's not a good atmosphere for learning, so we started a dress code. That ended the fashion race," Mrs. Jackson says. "It really stopped the teasing and conflicts."

 (READING 2) ### New Exhibit on Men's Skirts Opens at the Metropolitan Museum

Throughout Western history, women have borrowed men's clothing. Women wear pants, ties, and even men's suits. However, men have rarely worn women's clothing. One of the strongest taboos is against men wearing skirts. Skirts are considered inappropriate for men. A new exhibit at the Metropolitan Museum of Art called "Bravehearts: Men in Skirts" looks at this question.

David Thorndike, sociologist at the Modern Social Research Institute, says, "Men think if they wear a skirt, they will look feminine. That is absurd. Roman gladiators were very masculine and they wore skirts." He continues, "At one time, only men wore pants. However, today pants are unisex clothes. They are appropriate for both men and women. Women wear them all the time. If a man wants to wear masculine clothing, he should put on a real Scottish kilt."

The exhibit has examples of men's skirts in history. In addition, there are a number of skirts from well-known clothing designers. There is even a photograph of movie star Brad Pitt in a skirt. One male visitor said, "That skirt looks really comfortable. If Brad Pitt can wear it, why can't I?"

The exhibit will continue through February 8.

Cabbies Upset with Dress Code

EDINBURGH—Taxicab drivers in Edinburgh, Scotland, are upset about a strict new dress code that says they must wear flannel trousers, a shirt, and shoes.

Cabbies say the code is too restrictive. Furthermore, they complain that it takes away freedom to wear the national dress—including the Scottish kilt. Cabbie Jim Taylor, of the Edinburgh Street Taxi Association, says that cabbies will go to court if they are forced to follow the dress code.

Taylor remarks, "Most drivers already dress appropriately so there is absolutely no need for such a restrictive dress code. What if a driver wants to wear a kilt? According to this new dress code, he can't. After all, we are self-employed drivers. We are not city employees. It is unreasonable for the government to make us follow a dress code like this. No judge can tell us how to dress."

However, Phil Attridge, a member of the city council, disagreed. "We do not think the dress code is strict. Most drivers already follow it. We don't want drivers to wear jeans or shorts. Dress is important because drivers often go into hotels to pick up passengers—they should be well-dressed."

On the issue of kilts and national dress, Attridge added, "If a driver wants to wear some kind of national dress that is not in the code, he or she can ask permission."

He said a survey showed that 76 percent of cabbies and taxi owners wanted the dress code. According to sources, police officers are already enforcing the dress code, and one driver has already paid a fine for wearing corduroy trousers instead of flannel.

Reading Comprehension

Check Your Predictions

1. How good were your predictions on page 35?

Prediction	Not Accurate	Accurate
1		
2		
3		

2. If you found the answers to your questions, what were they?

_____

_____

_____

Check the Facts

Write *true* (T) or *false* (F) for each statement about the readings. Then go back to the readings and look for the answers you are unsure of.

READING 1

_____ 1. Young teenagers don't like to dress the same.

_____ 2. Dressing alike makes teenagers feel secure.

_____ 3. The *right* clothes are often expensive.

_____ 4. Teenagers sometimes laugh at students who wear school uniforms.

_____ 5. Dress codes cause problems in schools.

READING 2

_____ 1. The exhibit focuses on women wearing pants, and men wearing skirts.

_____ 2. According to an expert, men think that skirts are feminine.

_____ 3. There are skirts by modern designers in the exhibit.

_____ 4. Roman gladiators wore skirts.

_____ 5. No one complains when women wear men's clothes.

_____ 1. Cabbies are truck drivers.

_____ 2. The dress code says that cabbies must wear kilts.

_____ 3. Some cab drivers are unhappy about the dress code.

_____ 4. Under the dress code, cabbies are not allowed to wear jeans.

_____ 5. Cabbies who did not follow the dress code have to pay a fine.

Analyze

1. How is the dress code in the first article similar to the dress code in Reading 3? How is it different?

2. Is the situation about men wearing skirts more similar to the clothing situation in Reading 1 or Reading 2? Why?

Vocabulary Work

Guess Meaning from Context

1. The following names are all proper nouns. It is not necessary to understand every word in the name, but you should have an idea about what each group does from the words you do know. Write your ideas below.

   • **Edinburgh Street Taxi Association**

   _____

   • **The Modern Social Research Institute**

   _____

   • **The Metropolitan Museum of Art**

   _____

2. Work with a partner. Look back at the readings and try to guess the meanings of these words and phrases.

Word/Phrase	Reading	Meaning
fit in	1	
alike	1	
peer group	1	
taboo	2	
feminine	2	
gladiator	2	
masculine	2	
kilt	2 & 3	
fine	3	

3. Then turn to page 164 and match the meanings with the words.

4. Look at the words you guessed correctly. Look back at the reading. What clues did you use?

5. The words *flannel* and *corduroy* from Reading 2 are probably
   a. styles of trousers.
   b. kinds of cloth.
   c. fashion designers.

Guess Meaning from Related Words

1. Underline and use parts of the words you know to guess the meanings of these words.

Word/Phrase	Reading	Meaning
identical	1	
identity	1	
dress code	1 & 3	
unisex	2	
strict	3	
restrictive	3	
disagreed	3	

2. The word *judge* appears in Reading 1 and Reading 3. How are the meanings related? How are they different?

3. How are the words *appropriate*, *inappropriate*, and *appropriately* related in Readings 2 and 3?

Reading Skills

Understanding Cohesion

1. Identify the referents of the underlined words and phrases.

Fashion can be a lot of fun, but <u>it</u> has another side, too. Sometimes the
pressure of dressing in a certain way creates problems especially in families
with no money for expensive clothes. Some schools have found a solution
to <u>this problem</u>. <u>They</u> have a dress code or make students wear uniforms.
"Students were laughed at if <u>they</u> didn't have the right clothes. <u>That's</u> not a
good atmosphere for learning, so <u>we</u> started a dress code. <u>That</u> ended the
fashion race," Mrs. Jackson says. "<u>It</u> really stopped the teasing and conflicts."

1. _____   5. _____

2. _____   6. _____

3. _____   7. _____

4. _____   8. _____

2. In Reading 1, what is *"another side"* of fashion?

Discussion

1. Do you think having a dress code at schools is a good thing?
    Why or why not?

2. Do you think that the cabbie dress code is reasonable? Why
    or why not?

PART II

*The following reading is more difficult than the articles in Part I. Read it for the
main ideas. Do not worry if you cannot understand everything.*

Read It

Try to find the answers to these questions.

1. Why did the commission make the hijab illegal in schools?

2. Why do the Sikhs wear turbans?

 **READING**

First the Hijab, Then the Turban?

*After the ban on the Hijab,
will Sikhs be able to wear turbans?*

In 2004 the French government decided to ban all obvious religious symbols from public schools. As a result, Muslim girls could no longer wear the *hijab,* or the head scarf. Jews were not allowed to wear *yarmulkes,* or skullcaps. Even large Christian crosses were not permitted.

A special commission researched the question and made the recommendation to ban the religious clothing. Former government minister Bernard Stasi headed the group. He said that the members of the group consulted many different people—including teachers, religious leaders, sociologists, and politicians—before they made their decision.

The commission felt that conspicuous religious symbols set people apart and stop them from feeling truly *French.* By instituting this ban, the commission hopes that immigrants will become a more integral part of French society if they do not wear such clothing. Traditionally, newcomers from Africa and the Middle East have often been poorly integrated into French society.

However, this decision has upset other ethnic groups. For example, there are about 5,000 Sikhs in France. Being mostly lower middle class and thus having little access to mainstream French media, they did not know about the government commission. The commission was not aware of their concerns either. As a result, Sikhs never had the opportunity to testify in the hearings.

Several thousand Sikhs held a rally in Paris last week. They wanted to know if they have to take off their turbans. Or should they, as Luc Ferry, the education minister said, wear "see-through turbans." Sikh spokesmen argue that the turban is not a symbol of their religion. They wear turbans to cover their hair, which they never cut. Therefore, if they cannot wear turbans, their hair, which is the real symbol, will be uncovered.

"We feel undressed if we don't wear our turbans," said Simranjit Singh, a Sikh member of the Indian parliament who came to France—along with hundreds of people from all over Europe and America—for Saturday's rally. "It is humiliating to the core if we are made to take off our turbans."

The government has not yet made a decision on the legality of the turban.

Vocabulary Work

Guess Meaning from Related Words

1. Guess the meaning of these words.

    a. undressed _____   c. hearings _____

    b. newcomers _____   d. headed _____

2. Find a word related to the underlined word in the reading. Write the meaning.

	Related word	Meaning
a. To <u>recommend</u> means *to suggest.*	_____ means	_____
b. To <u>immigrate</u> means *to move to a new country.*	_____ means	_____
c. To <u>humiliate</u> means *to embarrass.*	_____ means	_____

Idea Exchange

Think about Your Ideas

1. What are the rules about your clothes?

	There are no restrictions	There is a formal dress code	There is an informal dress code
at home			
at school/work			
in public places			

2. What factors do you think about when deciding on proper clothing: fashion? safety? comfort? social norms? religion?

Talk about Your Ideas

1. Do you always wear what you want to? Do you ever have to follow a formal dress code? An informal dress code? When and why?

2. Do dress codes always make sense? If so, in what situations? What factors should we think about?

For CNN video activities about fashion, turn to page 171.

CHAPTER 5

WORK: Is it interfering with your life?

PREVIEW

Put these jobs into the appropriate categories.

actor	astronaut	chef	farmer	mechanic
architect	baker	coach	hotel manager	stockbroker
artist	banker	dentist	lawyer	zoologist

Jobs for people who:

. . . don't like to wear suits
or formal clothing.

_____

_____

_____

_____

. . . are very organized.

_____

_____

_____

_____

. . . like unpredictable days.

_____
_____
_____
_____

. . . love people.

_____
_____
_____
_____

. . . want to work with their hands.

_____
_____
_____
_____

PART I

Predict

Skim the three readings and make predictions.

1. Who are the Internet police?

2. What does a hurricane hunter do?

3. What kind of training do you need to be a disc jockey?

4. Which articles have quotations from people working in the field?

5. Write a question that you think each article may answer.

   _____
   _____
   _____

Read It

Read the articles. Look for the answers to your questions.

 **READING 1** The Internet Police

You're using the computer at work. After a while, you decide to take a break and go shopping—on the Internet. But when you click on your favorite shopping Web site, there's a big red hand on the screen. At the bottom of the screen, you see a warning from your company about unauthorized Web surfing.

So, who put it there? People like Ida Smith. Ms. Smith is a content specialist for a Web-filtering company. She spends her days surfing the Web. She is looking for sites that employers do not want their employees to visit. Her specific task is to find shopping, travel, and gambling sites. These sites are some of the places where employees may waste time at work. (Other content specialists look for sites on sex, drugs, and violence. There are 39 categories in all.) She also scans *white lists*—approved sites for children—to make sure that they have no links to naughty sites.

Special *spidering* programs actually do most of the work. These programs can search millions of pages in just a few minutes. But people like Ms. Smith provide a human review to make sure that pages are not blacklisted or white-listed by mistake.

Ms. Smith enjoys the work. "I love spending time on the Internet. I feel like I'm in touch with what people think and what they're doing," she says. However, she admits often taking a couple of aspirin when she gets home. "All that surfing gives me a headache," she explains.

An Interview with a Hurricane Hunter
by Joe LaTona

Last week I spoke with Karla Williams, a hurricane hunter from Miami, Florida.

JL: How did you obtain this job?
KW: I was working as a meteorologist. Then I saw a movie called *Storm Chasers.* It was about hurricane hunters—scientists who fly into hurricanes to do research. I thought that it would be a very interesting job. Then two months later I saw an ad for a hurricane researcher. I applied and got the job.

JL: What do you like most about being a hurricane hunter?
KW: I like working with the other scientists—it's a classroom in the sky. I also enjoy traveling around the world.

JL: What is an average day like?
KW: There are no average days in this job during hurricane season. The weather is constantly changing. You can never plan anything too far in advance. Of course, afterwards we work with the information we collect. Then it's pretty much 9 to 5 work for a few months.

JL: What is your educational and professional background?
KW: I received my bachelor's degree in meteorology from Penn State University, and then went to work as a meteorologist.

JL: What advice would you give someone who wanted to enter this field?
KW: Math and science. Math and science. Get a degree in meteorology and be willing to travel.

Disc Jockey

What the Job Is

Disc jockeys (DJs) introduce songs on the radio. They may also decide what music to play. While on the air, they comment on the music, weather, and traffic. DJs also announce and play music at clubs, dances, restaurants, and weddings. Some disc jockeys specialize in only one kind of music.

The Skills You Need

DJs need a pleasant and well-controlled voice, good timing, excellent pronunciation, and a strong grasp of correct grammar. Additionally, DJs should be able to speak *off the cuff* and to work under tight deadlines. The most successful announcers have a pleasing personality and voice with a likable style.

The Training You Should Have

Formal training in broadcasting from a college or technical school is valuable. Courses in English, public speaking, drama, and computer science are useful. Hobbies such as sports and music are also helpful.

The Salary You Can Expect

Salaries vary widely from $7,000 to $100,000+, depending on experience and market.

Reading Comprehension

Check Your Predictions

1. How good were your predictions?

Prediction	Not Accurate	Accurate
1		
2		
3		
4		

2. If you found the answers to your questions, what were they?

_____

_____

_____

_____

Check the Facts

Check (✓) the questions you can answer after reading once. Then go back and look for the answers that you are unsure of.

(READING 1)

_____ 1. What happens if employees go to an *illegal* site?

_____ 2. What kind of company does Ms. Smith work for?

_____ 3. What does she do?

_____ 4. What kinds of sites does she look for?

_____ 5. Why do companies want to block some Internet sites?

_____ 6. Does Ms. Smith like her job? What does she say?

(READING 2)

_____ 1. Who is answering the questions?

_____ 2. What does Karla like about her job?

_____ 3. How did she get her job?

_____ 4. Her job has two parts. What are they?

_____ 5. What did she study?

(READING 3)

_____ 1. What is an abbreviation for *disc jockey?*

_____ 2. Where do disc jockeys work?

_____ 3. What skills do disc jockeys need?

_____ 4. Should disc jockeys go to college? Why or why not?

_____ 5. How much money do disc jockey's make?

Analyze

Compare the jobs mentioned in the readings.
Which one . . .

is the most dangerous?   _____

requires the most education?   _____

would you enjoy the most?   _____

requires the least education?   _____

is probably for young people?   _____

Vocabulary Work

Guess Meaning from Context

1. There are several common phrases and idioms in the readings. Can you guess their meanings?

Phrase	Reading	Meaning
take a break	1	_____
waste time	1	_____
in touch with	1	_____
in advance	2	_____
pretty much	2	_____
on the air	3	_____
off the cuff	3	_____
public speaking	3	_____

2. Is the word *naughty* in Reading 1 good or bad? Why do you think so?

Guess Meaning from Related Words

1. Below are words from the readings. Write the parts that look like other words you already know. Then guess the meanings of the words.

Word	Reading	Contains	Meaning
blacklisted	1	_____	_____
white-listed	1	_____	_____
background	2	_____	_____
timing	3	_____	_____
well-controlled	3	_____	_____
personality	3	_____	_____
announcer	3	_____	_____
likable	3	_____	_____
pleasing	3	_____	_____
technical	3	_____	_____

2. Turn to page 164 and match the meanings with the words.

3. What is the relationship between these pairs of words?

meteorology	meteorologist
profession	professional
announce	announcer

Reading Skills

Understanding the Purpose of a Reading

All three readings contain information about a particular job. However, each writer had a different purpose.

1. Which article is meant to give readers a lot of information?

   Reading _____

   Why? _____

2. Which article is meant to entertain readers?

   Reading _____

   Why? _____

3. Which article is meant to interest readers in a certain career?

   Reading _____

   Why? _____

Discussion

1. Which, if any, of these jobs would you like to do? Why?
2. Which of these jobs would you least like to do? Why?

PART II

This reading is more difficult than the articles in Part I. Read it for the main ideas. Do not worry if you cannot understand everything.

Read It

Read to find the answers to these questions.

1. How is work more stressful today than it was before?
2. Why are workers feeling nervous?
3. Why do many people have jobs that they hate?
4. How can you create challenge on the job?
5. What can you do outside of work?
6. How can colleagues help?

 READING   Say Goodbye to the Monday Morning Blues

It's Sunday evening. The weekend is gone. Tomorrow is the start of another long workweek. Your head is already beginning to ache . . .

Many people feel so much stress at work that they hate going back on Monday morning after a weekend at home. They are fearful, anxious, and uncertain because work gives them little job security and heavy workloads. Peter Fielding, a Canadian psychologist, says, "There is no longer the feeling of being a long-term, valued employee. Just look at the newspaper and you read about layoffs, strikes, shutdowns." With downsizing, workers also have increased workloads. "We are all expected to do more with less and that's difficult," he explains.

Workers who used to have autonomy, freedom, and control now feel powerless. They are beginning to question the value of their work. "Professional identity is a real part of personal identity," says Nan Gardener, an unemployment counselor. "When you don't feel that you are making a significant and worthwhile contribution, it's hard to keep going."

Although the work climate today is difficult, there are ways for individuals to fight the stress.

Take back some control.

You may not be able to control events that happen around you, but you can control your response. Ask yourself, "Where can I get some job satisfaction and job challenge? What can I do with what I've got?" Try to find something each day that provides a challenge, even if it is just a different way of doing ordinary tasks. Challenge creates excitement. It motivates and revitalizes.

Balance work and play.

After many years of education, many people are unable to find a job in their field. Instead, they have to take any job to get a paycheck. The job may not be suited to their capabilities. It may not present the challenge they are looking for. If this describes your job, remember you are more than your occupation. Enrich your life in other areas. Involve yourself in activities outside of work. Gain strength from the areas in your life where things are going well. Realize that this job may be temporary and do the best job you can. Remember, too, many people don't have a job to hate.

Get support from colleagues.

We all need support from our colleagues in the workplace. Little things mean a lot, like potluck lunches and birthday celebrations. We also don't laugh as much as we used to in the workplace, yet a sense of humor can be vital. Decide that you will laugh at whatever you can laugh at and take advantage of the mutual support of colleagues.

Have realistic expectations.

With increased workloads and cutbacks, many people are feeling they can't do their best work. Keep your work in perspective. Look at the big picture and establish reasonable objectives. Prioritize and make lists. Do what you can each day, and recognize each accomplishment. Look at what you *can* achieve, not at what you can't.

Be cooperative.
In hard times, it is difficult to focus on the shared goals of employer and employee. Yet, maintaining an attitude of cooperation and a team approach can make your days more positive and rewarding.

Communicate, communicate, communicate!
Clear communication between management and staff is vital in these days of ongoing change. It is also important for management to invite input from staff on work issues, particularly those that will directly affect staff.

Vocabulary Work

Guess Meaning from Context

What do each of these words mean in the context of the reading?

1. downsizing _____
2. layoffs _____
3. strikes _____
4. shutdowns _____

Guess Meaning from Related Words

Decide if each word has a positive, negative, or neutral meaning.

1. autonomy _____
2. long-term _____
3. powerless _____
4. rewarding _____
5. significant _____
6. temporary _____
7. uncertain _____
8. valued _____
9. worthwhile _____

Reading Skills

Understanding Main Ideas

1. What is the writer's main point?
2. Who is this article written for?
3. Is the writer trying to persuade, explain, or describe something?

Idea Exchange

Think about Your Ideas

Number the five most important factors in choosing a career.

_____ salary

_____ amount of challenge

_____ amount of education or training necessary

_____ social status

_____ excitement

_____ possibility of advancement

_____ amount of free time

_____ amount of independence (autonomy)

_____ personal satisfaction

Talk about Your Ideas

1. What factors are most important when choosing a career? Why? What factors are not important to you at all? Why not?
2. Do you plan to work in one field for your entire life, or do you think you will change professions? Why or why not?

For CNN video activities about working too much, turn to page 172.

CHAPTER

Internet Dating: Is this really *YOUR* photo?

PREVIEW

Read these three true stories. Were these people wise or foolish? Discuss your answers.

Andre: I met my wife on the Internet. I liked her immediately because she was honest about her opinions. We talked online for more than a year. Then I drove 2,000 miles to meet her. We had a wonderful time. I moved across the country to be near her and we got married six months later.

Christie: My husband and I met through an Internet dating service. The first time we spoke, we talked online from 8 P.M. to 3 A.M. Then we talked on the phone until I had to leave for work. Two days later he came to visit. Two weeks later, we were married. He said, "Do you want to get married tonight?" I said, "No . . . but I'm off Tuesday." We were married that day in Alabama, just the two of us and the judge.

Elisa: I met a man on the Internet. He seemed great. We fell in love right away. He told me that he was 32 and a bachelor. Six months after we met, his wife called me. He was actually 42 and married with three kids!

PART I

Predict

Skim the two readings and make predictions.

1. Which article is probably more important to women than to men?
2. Skim Reading 1. Describe the kind of photograph that got the most replies.
3. Think of three possible rules for Internet dating that might be included in Reading 2.
4. Write a question for each article.

_____

_____

_____

_____

Read It

Read the article and look for the answers to your questions in Item 4 above.

READING 1

Reporter Discovers That Sex Sells
(What a Surprise . . .)

As you probably know, every Internet dating service asks you to fill out a profile about yourself, often including your job, hobbies, interests, and age. You can also put a picture next to your profile. Internet profiles with pictures get many more replies. Reporter Janice Walker decided to find out if people would pay more attention to her picture or to her profile. She sent the following profile to six different Internet dating sites:

> _My name is Kate, I am 35, work in the media, and have a great sense of humor. I enjoy travel and the arts. I am happy with my life, but I am missing that special someone._

Then she sent each one a different photograph of herself.

1. **Sexy Lady**   108 replies

   Janice put on a sexy dress and a lot of makeup. She didn't smile. This photo was the runaway favorite. Unfortunately, many of the replies were quite impolite. Almost all of the men only talked about her appearance.

2. **Happy and Healthy**   72 replies

   For this picture, Janice wore jeans and a T-shirt. This was the real her, so she was happy to get so many replies. Many men talked about the information in her profile. These men seemed like people she might go out with.

3. **Star Athlete**   41 replies

   Janice is not athletic, but she put on a tracksuit and stood next to a bicycle. She got a lot of responses from attractive, athletic men.

4. **All Business**   36 replies

   To look like a successful businesswoman, Janice wore a business suit and put on glasses. Few men of her age were interested. Most of the respondents talked about their salaries, their cars, and their successful careers.

5. **Sophisticated Lady**   20 replies

   For this photo, Janice wore her best dress and put her hair up. She wanted to look high-class. However, not many men were interested. The youngest was 39 and the oldest was 55.

6. **Little Girl**   4 replies

   In this photograph, Janice wore a pink sweater and held a stuffed bear. There were almost no responses. Two of the men who replied were in their fifties. Both said she looked sweet, and one even said she reminded him of his daughter.

Janice was disappointed that the results were very predictable. Though her profile showed that she was an intelligent woman, most of the men responded to the pictures—not to the words.

READING 2 Rules for Internet Dating

Every time that you meet someone new, you take a risk. If you meet in a grocery store, in a museum, or in an Internet chat room, you have to protect yourself. The following rules apply to Internet dating.

1. Use Common Sense
Don't give out personal information such as your name, telephone number, or address until you are comfortable. You may want to use your first name only or use a fictitious name until you feel safe. When you feel safe enough to talk on the telephone, don't give out your home number. Get his or her number, or give them your work number, or your cellular phone number. Get together in a public place for the first date. Tell people where you are going or bring along some friends.

2. _____
Tell the truth. If you send a photograph, make sure it's up-to-date. Telling the truth will avoid anger and disappointment later.

3. _____
Get to know someone before getting romantic. Send e-mail messages for a while before you talk on the telephone or meet face-to-face. If he or she won't wait until you're comfortable, you should wonder why.

4. _____
You can meet liars and cheaters on the Internet just like you can in real life. Look for the signs. Beware of Internet friends who try to persuade you to do something or make a lot of promises. Save your messages. If you think someone's lying, you can look back at what they said before. Previous messages may give you a clue.

5. _____
Before getting close to someone online, find out if the person is _real._ Ask for his or her home phone number, work number, and even references. It's easy to create a fake identity in cyberspace.

6. _____
Internet dating can be as exciting as dating in person. Enjoy yourself but move slowly. Don't jump right into romance.

Reading Comprehension

Check Your Predictions

1. Look back at your questions in the Predict section. How good were your predictions?

Prediction	Not Accurate	Accurate
1		
2		
3		

2. If you found the answers to your questions from Item 4, what were they?

_____

_____

_____

_____

_____

_____

Check the Facts

Check (✓) the questions you can answer after reading once. Then go back and look for the answers that you are unsure of.

READING 1

_____ 1. What did Janice Walker want to find out?

_____ 2. What did she send to each Internet dating service?

_____ 3. How was each one different?

_____ 4. Which picture was the most popular?

_____ 5. Was she surprised at the results? Why or why not?

_____ 1. Where should you meet an Internet date in person for the first time?

_____ 2. Why is it important to tell the truth?

_____ 3. What should you do with the messages you receive? Why?

_____ 4. How can you find out if a person is *real*?

Analyze

1. How does the writer of Reading 1 feel about online dating services?

2. What other rules might the writer of Reading 2 add to the list?

Vocabulary Work

Guess Meaning from Context

1. Work with a partner. Look back at the readings and try to guess the meaning of these words.

Word/Phrase	Reading	Meaning
profile	1	
tracksuit	1	
risk	2	
anger	2	
up-to-date	2	
face-to-face	2	
persuade	2	
previous	2	
fake identity	2	

2. Then turn to page 164 and match the meanings with the words.

3. Look at the words you guessed correctly. Look back at the reading. What clues did you use?

4. Look back at Reading 2. Are *liars* and *cheaters* good or bad? Why do you think so?

Guess Meaning from Related Words

1. Underline the part or parts of the word that you know. Then guess the meaning of the whole word.

    runaway   _____

    impolite   _____

    sports-minded   _____

    predictable   _____

2. Look for the words *disappointed* in Reading 1 and *disappointment* in Reading 2. How are they related?

Understanding Two- and Three-Word Verbs

Look back at these two- and three-word verbs from Reading 2.

Write another sentence with each one.

1. go out with   _____
2. give out   _____
3. get together   _____
4. bring along   _____
5. make sure   _____
6. get to know   _____
7. beware of   _____
8. look back at   _____
9. find out   _____
10. jump into   _____

Reading Skills

Using Subtitles

Both Readings 1 and 2 are lists. In Reading 1, each item in the list has a subtitle. How do these subtitles relate to the information that follows? As a reader, should you pay attention to the subtitles? Why or why not?

Summarizing Main Ideas

Reading 2 is a numbered list of rules for Internet dating. The rules summarize the explanations. They are the main ideas. Read paragraphs 2–6. Write a rule for each one.

Discussion

1. Do you think online dating is a good way to meet people? Why or why not?

2. Do you know anyone who has met someone online? What happened?

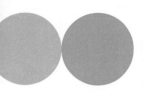

PART II

This reading is more difficult than the articles in Part I. Read it for the main ideas. Do not worry if you cannot understand everything.

Read It

Read to find the answers to these questions.

1. Find at least one advantage and one disadvantage of online dating.

2. How did people meet and marry 20 years ago?

3. Why don't people meet in the same ways that they used to?

 READING Online Dating Goes Mainstream

Patricia Costello, 33, e-mailed 120 men in her first four months of Internet dating. She talked to 20 of them on the telephone at least once and met 11 in person. Of these, she dated four several times and then realized she had not found *the one.*

One of the first lessons that subscribers to Internet dating sites learn is that life partners are difficult to find. But Ms. Costello isn't ready to give up. She is convinced that she has a better chance to find her life partner in cyberspace than in the real world.

Online dating is rapidly becoming a normal part of single life for adults of all ages in the United States. More than 45 million Americans visited online dating sites last month, according to comScore Media Metrix, a Web tracking service. Although the Internet has a reputation as a meeting place for people interested in casual sex, a majority of subscribers now say that they are looking for a serious relationship.

There are still many stories about liars. Many online daters are married and don't admit it. In fact, people are almost expected to lie a little or exaggerate their good qualities. Nonetheless, singles say that the Internet is still better than singles bars, dates set up by friends, or church groups for meeting other singles.

"My brother told me to take a dance class," said David Collins, 28, who met his fiancée, Sharon West, 27, on Match.com. "I tried it and met some nice people, but no one that I wanted to go out with."

"The traditional ways for getting people together are not working as well as they did before," said Linda Frankel, a sociology professor at the University of Southern Idaho. "There's a need for something new, and the Internet is filling that need."

"Twenty or thirty years ago, most American couples met in high school or college," Professor Frankel explained. "But people now marry at an older age, and there have not been any social institutions to replace the traditional ones—local communities, families, and schools. The Internet may be the answer."

Daniel Weston, author of the article "Find the Mate You Want Now," agrees. "The Internet not only allows you to meet people, but it allows you to choose from thousands of them. If you work hard enough, you can find the exact kind of person you are looking for."

Of course, Internet dating isn't perfect. Online daters often complain that it is difficult to judge physical chemistry through computer communication. "Certain things look really good on paper," said Regina Coughlin, a computer consultant in Manhattan. "Then, in real life, it's a completely different story."

After a few disappointing meetings, many online daters just quit. Those who find partners say they often think that they might find someone better—if they just looked through a few hundred more profiles.

Vocabulary Work

Guess Meaning from Related Words

Guess the meaning of these compound nouns and phrases.

life partner _____

physical chemistry _____

singles bars _____

in person _____

Reading Skills

Understanding Cohesion

1. What do the underlined phrases refer to?

    Patricia Costello, 33, e-mailed 120 men in her first four months of Internet dating. She talked to 20 *of them* on the telephone at least once and met 11 in person. *Of these*, she dated four several times and then realized she had not found *the one*.

2. Who does *the one* refer to?

Idea Exchange

Think about Your Ideas

1. Check (✓) the ways people in your culture meet.

    _____ through family

    _____ through friends

    _____ at school

    _____ at work

    _____ at places of worship (church, temple, mosque)

    _____ through personals ads

    _____ in bars and clubs

    _____ other _____

    _____

2. Write an Internet profile about yourself.

_____

_____

_____

_____

_____

_____

_____

Talk about Your Ideas

1. Compare the way people in your culture traditionally meet with meeting people on the Internet. What are the advantages and disadvantages of both? Are traditions in your culture starting to change? If so, how?

2. What would you look for in someone's personal profile if you wanted to date online?

For CNN video activities about internet dating, turn to page 173.

CHAPTER 7

ANGER: I'M NOT ANGRY!

YOU'RE ANGRY!

PREVIEW

Discuss the answers to these questions.

1. Match the statistics. Use the percentages in the box.

| 12% | 17% | 23% | 39% | 52% | 80% |

   a. What percentage of Americans say that they hide their anger?
   _____

   b. What percentage of Americans say that they have hit someone in anger?
   _____

   c. What percentage of Americans admit that they have destroyed someone's property in anger? _____

2. When do you get angry?

3. What do you do when you get angry?

4. Do you think that violence is more common today than it was 20 years ago? Why or why not?

Answers to page 67, Question 1: a. 39%   b. 23%   c. 17%

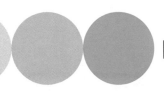

PART I

Predict

Skim the three readings and make predictions.

1. Which readings will teach you something about anger?

2. What are some ways to manage anger?

3. Which reading tells a story?

4. Write a question that you think each article may answer.

_____

_____

_____

Read It

Read the following three articles. Look for the answers to your questions.

How Angry Are You?

Everyone gets angry sometimes. Take this short quiz to find out how much anger affects you. Check the correct column.

	Almost never	Sometimes	Often	Almost always
1. I get angry easily.				
2. I get very, very angry.				
3. I get angry at other people's stupid mistakes.				
4. I feel angry when I am not treated fairly.				
5. I say hurtful things when I get angry.				
6. I get angry when people criticize me.				
7. When I get angry, I feel like hitting someone.				
8. I get angry when I am driving.				
9. Anger gives me a headache.				
10. When I get angry, I feel depressed.				

Your Anger Score

Almost never   = 1 point

Sometimes   = 2 points

Often   = 3 points

Almost always = 4 points

High Anger	Moderate Anger	Low Anger
22–40	15–21	10–14

People with high scores have heart attacks 2.7 times more often than people with low scores.

READING 2   Control Your Anger—Don't Let It Control You

Anger is a normal emotion. However, some people can't control or manage their anger. If anger is affecting your enjoyment of life, your work, or your relationships, then you may need help.

Some Advice for Anger Management
- Exercise regularly. It can help reduce tension and stress.
- Try some relaxation techniques. You can meditate, listen to soft music, or practice slow, deep breathing.
- Admit feelings of anger. Learn to recognize the signs of anger in yourself so that you can take action early.
- When you feel yourself getting angry, leave the situation.
- Avoid drinking alcohol, driving a car, or operating machinery when you are angry.
- Talk about your feelings with someone you trust.

 READING 3   The Swami and the Snake

On the train to Brindavan a Swami was sitting beside a common man. The common man asked, "Swami, I know you are a holy man, but have you mastered anger?"

"I have."

"Do you mean to say that you never get angry?"

"No, I don't."

"You mean you can control your anger?"

"Yes, I can."

"So, you do not feel anger."

"I do not."

"Is this the truth, Swami?"

"It is."

After a minute, the man asked again, "Do you really feel that you have controlled your anger?"

"I have, as I told you," the Swami answered.

"Then do you mean to say, you never feel anger, even . . ."

"You are going on and on—what do you want?" the Swami shouted. "Are you a fool? When I have told you . . ."

"Oh, Swami, this is anger. You have not mas—"

"Ah, but I have," the Swami interrupted. "Have you not heard about the story of the snake? Let me tell you. . . ."

"On a path near a village in Bengal, there lived a cobra who used to bite people on their way to the temple. Everyone in the village became fearful, and many of them stopped going to the temple. The Swami Ramala lived in that temple. He was a great swami, and he decided to use his powers to end the problem. He went out to the jungle and called the snake to him. The Swami Ramala then told the snake that it was wrong to bite people. He made him promise that he would never do it again. The snake agreed. People soon realized that the snake wasn't dangerous anymore. It was not long before the village boys were pulling the poor snake along behind them as they ran laughing. When the Swami Ramala passed that way again, he met the snake. The snake crawled up to the Swami Ramala, who exclaimed, 'You are bleeding. Tell me what happened.' The snake said, 'No one is afraid of me now and the children treat me very badly.'

'I told you not to *bite*,' said the Swami, 'but I did not tell you not to *hiss*.' "

Reading Comprehension

Check Your Predictions

1. How good were your predictions?

Prediction	Not Accurate	Accurate
1		
2		
3		

2. If you found the answers to your questions, what were they?

_____

_____

_____

Check the Facts

READING 1

Check (✓) the questions you can answer after reading once. Then go back and look for the answers that you are unsure of.

_____ 1. According to the quiz, what kinds of things make people angry?

_____ 2. What do some people do when they get angry?

_____ 3. What are some physical or mental results of getting angry?

_____ 4. Which is better for your health—a high score or a low score?

READING 2

Write *true* (T) or *false* (F). When the statement is false, what is the correct answer?

_____ 1. You must always control your anger.

_____ 2. Stress can make you angry.

_____ 3. Loud music will not decrease your anger.

_____ 4. When you are angry, drinking alcohol is helpful.

_____ 5. You should notice the signs that you are getting angry.

_____ 6. Talking to someone can make you feel less angry.

READING 3

Check (✓) the questions you can answer after reading once. Then go back and look for the answers that you are unsure of.

_____ 1. Is a swami more like a priest or a doctor?

_____ 2. Why did the swami on the train get annoyed?

_____ 3. How did the snake in the story make the villagers afraid?

_____ 4. What did Swami Ramala ask the snake to do?

_____ 5. What happened to the snake?

_____ 6. What did Swami Ramala tell the snake to do in the end?

Analyze

1. How would the swami on the train score on the anger quiz?
2. Would the Swami Ramala and the writer of Reading 2 agree?
3. How are hissing and biting the same as getting angry?

Vocabulary Work

Guess Meaning from Context

1. Work with a partner. Look back at the readings and try to guess the meaning of these words.

Word	Reading	Meaning
moderate	1	
manage	2	
criticize	1	
tension	2	
temple	3	
cobra	3	
hiss	3	

2. Then turn to page 165 and match the meanings with the words.
3. Look at the words you guessed correctly. Look back at the readings. What clues did you use?

Guess Meaning from Related Words

1. Underline the parts of the words that you know. Then guess the meaning of the whole word.

   hurtful   _____

   enjoyment   _____

   machinery   _____

   relaxation   _____

2. Explain the difference between these related words.

anger	angry
meditate	meditation
depressed	depression
manage	management

Reading Skills

Finding Referents

Look back at Reading 3. Write the noun that each underlined pronoun refers to. Write _X_ if it does not refer to any noun.

Referent	Noun
1. . . . and many of <u>them</u> stopped . . .	_____
2. . . . called the snake to <u>him</u>.	_____
3. <u>He</u> made <u>him</u> promise	_____ _____
that <u>he</u> would never do <u>it</u> again.	_____ _____
4. <u>It</u> was not long before . . .	_____

Discussion

1. Think of another item to add to the anger quiz.
2. Think of another item to add to the anger management advice.
3. Can you think of a time that you "hissed" but didn't "bite"?

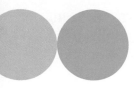

PART II

This reading is more difficult than the selections in Part I. Read it for the main ideas. Do not worry if you cannot understand everything.

Read It

Read to find the answers to these questions.

1. Write the names of the cultures where expressions of anger are appropriate.

2. Write the names of the cultures where expressions of anger are inappropriate.

 READING   Anger around the World

Attitudes about expressing anger vary from culture to culture. In some cultures, almost any sign of anger is inappropriate. In others, people use anger as a way of extending relationships. The differences in attitudes about anger can cause a lot of cross-cultural miscommunication. For example, anthropologist Jean Briggs spent 17 months as the adopted daughter of an Utku Eskimo family. During this time, she discovered if she expressed anger in a way that was appropriate in the United States, the Eskimos thought that she was childish. As a result, she learned not to show her anger.

The Utku are just one example of a culture that dislikes signs of anger. Finnish people also believe that expressions of anger show a lack of self-control. This attitude can make them seem very peaceful. For example, road rage is a problem in many countries, but not in Finland. There, experts say, a car accident doesn't make people angry. The drivers politely exchange information and then go on. And no one complains when a bus breaks down. The passengers simply get off and wait for the next one.

(Continued on page 76)

Such behavior would not happen in the United States where expressing anger is accepted—even expected. The problem occurs when people from cultures where anger is acceptable visit countries where it is not. For example, if an American visiting England complained in a tone of voice that would be effective at home, no one would pay attention. They would see him as just another impolite American. This is because the English usually avoid showing anger unless the situation is extremely serious.

Avoidance of public anger is also common in China and Japan. In both of these cultures, the expression of anger is unacceptable and destructive. This attitude is very different from the one in the United States, where many people believe that not expressing anger can lead to depression, alcoholism, drug addiction, or even violence. In countries that don't express anger, most people would think this idea was ridiculous or even dangerous.

However, in some other cultures, anger is more lightly received and forgotten than in the United States. Americans traveling in the Middle East or some Mediterranean countries are often surprised by the amount of anger they see and hear. They do not realize that people in these countries express their anger and then forget it. Even the people who are on the receiving end of the anger usually do not remember it for long. In fact, in these cultures, fierce arguments and confrontation can be positive signs of friendliness and engagement. Here, again, is a good deal of opportunity for misunderstanding and resentment between cultures.

Vocabulary Work

Guess Meaning from Related Words

1. Find other forms of these words in the reading.

   a. accept   _____

   _____

   b. avoid   _____

   c. effect   _____

   d. express   _____

   e. communicate   _____

   f. destroy   _____

   g. understand   _____

   h. friend   _____

   i. polite   _____

   j. violent   _____

2. Are these words positive or negative? Why do you think so?

   a. ridiculous   _____

   b. confrontation   _____

   c. resentment   _____

3. Can you guess the meaning of *road rage*?

   _____

   _____

Idea Exchange

Think about Your Ideas

1. Write 3–5 ways of expressing anger that are acceptable in your culture.

   _____

   _____

   _____

   _____

   _____

2. Number the items above from the least serious (1) to the most serious (3–5).

3. Write two ways of showing anger that would *not* be acceptable in your culture.

   _____

   _____

Talk about Your Ideas

1. How does your culture deal with anger? Does it allow expressions of anger or not? What problems, if any, does this cause?

2. People in some countries take courses to help them control their anger. At least one man in Finland is teaching people how to be more angry. Do you think that people can learn to control or express their anger in a class? Why or why not?

For CNN video activities about anger, turn to page 174.

CHAPTER 8

Psychics: What do they know that we don't?

PREVIEW

Discuss the answers to these questions.

1. What astrological sign are you? Do you know the characteristics of people with your sign?

2. Do you read your horoscope in the newspaper? If so, does it influence your decisions?

3. Have you ever been to a fortune teller? If not, would you ever go? Why or why not?

PART I

Predict

Skim the three readings and make predictions.

1. Which reading or readings are in favor of psychics?

2. Which reading is trying to persuade you to do something?

3. Which reading or readings give advice?

4. Which reading talks about something that has happened?

5. Write a question for each reading.

_____

_____

_____

Read It

Read the articles and look for the answers to your questions.

 READING 1

Cyberpsychic:
The Answers You Need When You Need Them

Welcome and thank you for choosing Cyberpsychic. This is a service that can truly change your life. We offer fast, accurate, and confidential readings on any subject you want—love, sex, money, or career. At last, you will be able to see your own future.

Analyzing Your Reading

For your reading, you will ask our psychic a question about one aspect of your life. In most cases, the answer you receive will be clear and easy to understand. However, in some cases, you may not receive a direct answer. This usually happens when the psychic talks directly to your unconscious mind. The psychic can see what is in your unconscious mind without your telling her. If this is the case, the psychic's meaning will become clear in time. If the answer seems complex or confusing, it may mean that your situation is far more complicated than you know.

Why We Are the Best!

Many psychic services charge as much as $50, $75, or even $100 for a single reading, Our fee is ONLY $14.95! How can we do this? We use advanced Internet software. This allows us to complete your reading and send it to you quickly and efficiently. You won't have to sit and wait. And when your reading arrives, you will be able to analyze it for as long as you want.

So, sign up with Cyberpsychic today. Your future is waiting for you.

Skeptics Defeat Psychics

TORONTO, CANADA—A Toronto-area skeptics society recently challenged local psychics to prove their abilities. The OSSCI (Ontario Skeptics Society for Critical Inquiry) offered $1,000 to anyone who could identify three common items in sealed boxes. The $1,000 Psychic Challenge was held November 2, 2002. Many local people say that they have psychic powers, so it seemed likely that at least one of them would win the money. So how did the crazies do? When the boxes were opened, there were no correct answers. No one was able to identify the three items. In fact, none of the supposed psychics could identify even *one* item.

The cardboard boxes were displayed on a table behind a rope. A guard watched to make sure that no one touched them. People had to look at the boxes from six feet away. They only knew that the objects were common items that most adults or adolescents would recognize. When they believed they knew what the items were, they wrote their answers on a form.

The boxes were opened in front of a small crowd—some hopeful, some skeptical. The items were a tangerine, a glove, and a roll of toilet paper. OSSCI is now working on a more extensive Psychic Challenge with a larger cash award—$10,000. They hope that more powerful psychics will take the test. However, after the results of the first test, Toronto-area skeptics are confident their money will be safe.

Finding a Real Psychic

So, how do you know if a psychic is genuine or not? It isn't easy. Although many experiments have been done to prove or disprove psychic powers, the results are usually unsatisfactory and inconclusive. Various organizations have offered $1,000,000 to anyone who can prove that they have psychic powers. Unfortunately, none of the psychics who have tried have won the prize money. There is good reason to be careful if you are looking for a psychic.

Here is some helpful advice.

Be suspicious of the following "tricks":

- **Unrealistic claims.** If the psychic promises to tell you winning lottery numbers or find a husband or wife for you, don't use him or her.
- **Expensive phone lines.** The person on the phone will try to lengthen your conversation for as long as possible because the longer you talk, the more you pay.
- **Cold reading.** Some psychics claim that they can tell people about their lives by just looking at them and concentrating. This technique is often helped by the subject's willingness to believe in the psychic's powers.
- **Warnings of death.** Real psychics will not tell you this sort of information.

In addition, real psychics will be happy to answer questions before you pay for a reading. They will also allow you to record the reading. Then you will be able to listen to it again. Make sure that you tell the psychic what you want to know about. Be specific.

Genuine psychics may have some form of training or be a member of an organization such as the College of Psychic Studies in London. However, some psychics work from home and don't have any qualifications, so you have to rely on your own judgment. Word of mouth can be another good way of finding a good psychic.

Reading Comprehension

Check Your Predictions

1. How good were your predictions?

Prediction	Not Accurate	Accurate
1		
2		
3		
4		

2. If you found the answers to your questions, what were they?

    _____

    _____

    _____

Check the Facts

Check (✓) the questions you can answer after reading once. Then go back and look for the answers that you are unsure of.

READING 1

_____ 1. How can you contact Cyberpsychic?

_____ 2. What can you ask questions about?

_____ 3. What may be the problem if you don't understand the answer?

_____ 4. What are some reasons that Cyberpsychic is better than other services?

READING 2

_____ 1. Do skeptics believe in psychic ability?

_____ 2. What did the skeptics offer the psychics?

_____ 3. How many people guessed correctly?

_____ 4. Were the skeptics disappointed?

_____ 5. What are the skeptics going to do next?

_____ 1. How have people tried to find real psychics?

_____ 2. Should you use a telephone psychic? Why or why not?

_____ 3. Will a real psychic promise to make you rich?

_____ 4. Are cold readings valid?

_____ 5. Have all real psychics gone to school?

Analyze

1. Use the criteria in Reading 3 to judge the Cyberpsychic in Reading 1. What are your conclusions?

2. Why don't real psychics do cold readings?

3. What kind of psychics work at Cyberpsychic?

4. Would the skeptics agree with the advice in Reading 3?

Vocabulary Work

Guess Meaning from Context

1. a. Work with a partner. Look back at the readings and try to guess the meaning of these words.

Word	Reading	Meaning
accurate	1	_____
confusing	1	_____
skeptic	2	_____

b. The words *complex* and *simple* are antonyms. Write an antonym for each word.

inexpensive   _____

unfortunately   _____

young   _____

c. The word *cold* is used in an unusual way in Reading 3. What does it mean? How is this meaning related to its normal meaning?

2. Then turn to page 165 and match the meanings with the words.

3. Look at the words you guessed correctly. Look back at the reading. What clues did you use?

Guess Meaning from Related Words

1. Underline the part of the word or phrase that you know. Then guess the meaning of the whole word.

   a. confident   _____

   b. confidential _____

   c. reading   _____

   d. unconscious _____

   e. unsatisfactory _____

   f. strengthen   _____

   g. expectation _____

2. How are the following pairs of words related?

   a. psychic   psychics

   _____

   b. skeptic   skeptical

   _____

   c. prove   disprove

   _____

Reading Skills

Detecting Bias

When writers want to influence people, they often misrepresent facts or leave out important information. Therefore, it is very important that readers evaluate critically as they are reading.

Look back at the readings. Decide if each reading has a bias. How do you know? Find words, phrases, or sentences that support your opinions.

_____

_____

_____

Discussion

1. Do these readings make it more or less likely that you will visit a psychic?
2. Should the government regulate psychics?

PART II

This reading is more difficult than the articles in Part I. Read it for the main ideas. Do not worry if you cannot understand everything.

Read It

Read to find the answers to these questions.

1. Does the writer believe in psychic powers? How do you know?
2. What tools can you use to make accurate predictions about people?
3. How can the subject help you succeed?
4. What is *fishing*?
5. Should you let the subject talk a lot? Why or why not?

Your Guide to *Cold Readings*

Psychics use *cold readings* to convince people of their powers. In cold readings, psychics tell their subjects things that "they couldn't have known." Actually, there are a number of simple tricks that they use to accomplish this amazing feat. You can learn these tricks, too.

Study this guide to cold reading. Then amaze your friends with your psychic powers!

1. Remember that the key ingredient of a successful character reading is confidence.

If you look and act as if you believe in what you are doing, you will be able to sell even a bad reading to most subjects.

2. Make use of the latest polls and surveys.

Probability and statistics enter the picture in many ways. For example the most common beginning letter for men's names is *J*; *M* is the most common for women's names. Knowing this information, you can tell your subject, "I see a woman in your life. Her name begins with *M*." The subject is bound to know someone whose name begins with that letter.

3. Set the stage for your reading.

Be modest about your talents. Make no excessive claims.

4. Get the subject's cooperation in advance.

Be sure to tell the subject that success of the reading depends on his or her cooperation. Explain that the subject must try to fit the reading to his or her own life. This tactic helps you in two ways. If the reading doesn't click, it's the subject's fault—not yours! And the subject will always be trying to help you. Remember—a good reader enables the subject to make sense of their own statements.

5. Use a gimmick, such as Tarot cards, a crystal ball, palm reading, etc.

Use of props serves two valuable purposes. First, it creates a mysterious atmosphere. Second, and more importantly, it gives you time to think of your next question or statement.

6. Make statements that are true for almost everyone.

Most people would agree with the following statement: "I see that you have financial issues that you have to take care of." Who doesn't? You can replace the word *financial* with *sexual* or *work* or *relationship*. Almost everyone has areas of concern with these issues.

7. Use your observations to begin guessing.

Carefully note the subject's age, clothes, jewelry, behavior, and speech. Careful observation will allow you to make accurate predictions from the very beginning. For example, if the subject lives in the north and looks wealthy, then you might say, "I see palm trees near the water." Nearly everyone in the north has taken or is thinking of taking a beach vacation. The subject will think you are correct, especially if you don't mention the past or future.

8. Use the technique of *fishing*.

Fishing is a way to get the subject to tell you about himself or herself. You rephrase what he or she has told you and feed it back to the subject. You can say things like, "I'm getting the feeling that . . ." or "I want to say that . . ." These are not direct questions, but they usually produce a response. Often the subject does not even realize that he or she has given you any information. After a short delay, you can repeat what the subject has told you. Your audience will be amazed.

9. Learn to be a good listener.

During a reading, the subject will want to talk about his or her life. Good readers allow the client to talk at will. On one occasion, I observed a tea leaf reader. The subject actually spent 75 percent of the time talking. Afterward I questioned the subject about the reading. She insisted that she had not spoken!

10. Remember the Golden Rule—always tell the subject what you would want to hear about yourself.

People are more likely to recognize themselves when positive qualities are mentioned, such as "You are generous" or "You are creative." People are less likely to agree when you say "You are selfish" or "You are self-centered"— no matter how true!

Vocabulary Work

Look back at the reading and try to guess the meaning of these words.

1. key _____

2. subject _____

3. probability _____

4. cooperation _____

5. mysterious _____

6. delay _____

Reading Skills

Understanding Idioms

An idiom is an expression that does not mean the same as the individual words. The words "to hit the roof" say "to hit against the top of a house," but the idiom actually means "to become very angry." For example: "He hit the roof when he saw the $300 phone bill."

Look for the following idioms in the reading. Guess the meaning for each word or group of words and write it on the line.

1. to sell _____

2. enter the picture _____

3. fit _____

4. click _____

5. atmosphere _____

6. feed it back _____

Idea Exchange

Think about Your Ideas

1. In your opinion, what is the evidence in favor of psychics?

   _____   _____

   _____   _____

2. In your opinion, what is the evidence against psychics?

   _____   _____

   _____   _____

3. Have you ever . . .

   _____ visited a psychic or a fortune teller?

   _____ gone to a palm reader?

   _____ read your horoscope in the newspaper?

   _____ gone to a tarot card reader?

   _____ called a psychic hotline?

   _____ other _____

4. Would you ever . . .

   _____ visit a psychic or a fortune teller?

   _____ go to a palm reader?

   _____ read your horoscope in the newspaper?

   _____ go to a tarot card reader?

   _____ call a psychic hotline?

   _____ other _____

Talk about Your Ideas

1. Do you believe that some people have psychic power? Why or why not?

2. Do you have any experiences with psychics, astrology, etc.?

3. Have you ever had a experience that might have been psychic?

For CNN video activities about psychics and psychic power, turn to page 175.

CHAPTER 9

BEAUTY:
MIRROR, MIRROR,
ON THE WALL . . .

PREVIEW

Discuss the answers to these questions.

1. The title of this chapter is part of a quote, "Mirror, mirror, on the wall, who's the fairest of them all?" What famous character in a Walt Disney movie said this? What was she talking about?

2. Do the following statistics surprise you? Do you know anyone who has had plastic surgery?

   • Since 1992, cosmetic surgery has increased 175 percent.

   • Americans spend more than $30 billion a year on cosmetics such as lipstick and eye makeup.

PART I

Predict

Skim the three readings and make predictions.

1. Which readings give information based on a scientific study?
2. Which reading describes a television show?
3. Which reading talks about the advantages of being attractive?
4. Which reading tries to persuade readers to do something?
5. Which article will give you the most interesting information?
6. Which article has information about both men and women?
7. Write a question that you think each article may answer.

_____

_____

_____

Read It

Read the articles. Look for the answers to your questions.

 READING 1 Why Appearance Is Important

We are all more concerned with our appearance. For most of us, this concern is not simply vanity. *Vanity* means having too much pride in one's appearance. On the other hand, concern about appearance is quite understandable because attractive people have many advantages in our society. According to the Social Issues Research Centre in Oxford, England, studies show that

1. attractive children are more popular;
2. teachers give attractive children better grades;
3. attractive job applicants have a better chance of getting hired. They also get higher salaries;
4. people generally believe that physically attractive people have other desirable characteristics such as intelligence, competence, confidence, and morality. (The good princess is always beautiful; the wicked stepmother is always ugly.)

Therefore, it is not surprising that physical attraction is of great importance to us. This concern with appearance did not begin with modern Western culture. Every period of history has had standards of beauty. For example, one hundred years ago in China, people thought that women should have very small feet. To achieve this ideal, girls had their feet bound to stop their natural growth. However, even though appearance has been important in every age and every culture, it has not always been as important as it is today. Western societies today are obsessed with physical appearance. Some people believe that science and the media have caused this obsession.

 (READING 2)   Would You Like an Extreme Makeover?

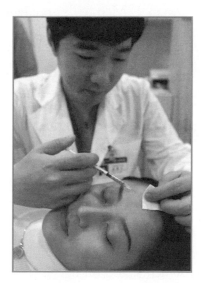

Have you ever dreamed of having a prettier smile, a more beautiful nose, a flatter stomach, more beautiful hair, or just *more* hair. Whatever your dream is, you could win it on *Extreme Makeover.*

At *Extreme Makeover,* our motto is, "We'll stop at nothing to change ordinary into extraordinary!" Each episode features two lucky candidates. First, the viewers see them before we have done anything to them. Then, they watch them undergo various makeover procedures. This is no ordinary hair, makeup, and clothes makeover. Our *Extreme* team of specialists includes plastic surgeons, eye surgeons, cosmetic dentists, hair stylists, fashion consultants, makeup experts, and personal trainers. They guide and educate the participants through each stage of the makeover process. Finally, the audience gets to see the result—when the candidates reintroduce themselves to their families and friends. Thousands of people apply to be the lucky two by writing to the TV show and describing their physical flaws. Next time it could be you!

READING 3   Are Women Still the *Fair* Sex?

Studies find that men are worrying about their appearance, too.

When women are called the *fair* sex, the word is used in its old meaning of *pretty*— not today's common meaning of *open-minded.* Traditionally, women worried about their appearance. Men were more concerned with being strong and powerful. But men are becoming more and more concerned with the way that they look. Research from the Canadian Psychological Association shows that 75 percent of men today don't like how they look. And they're trying to fix their appearance. Men with gray hair are dying it. Men who are losing their hair are paying thousands of dollars to grow it back. Men are also using plastic surgery to fix their noses and remove fat. And just as women increase the size of their breasts with implants, men are now getting bicep implants to make their muscles look larger.

Why are they doing this? No one is certain. On the Canadian Psychological Association survey, men gave three reasons for wanting to be more attractive:

1. to get a better job
2. to be more athletic
3. to allure women

Mike Lyons, a gym manager in Chicago, doesn't believe these reasons. He says that men, like women, are unhappy with their appearance because they see *ideal* men in movies, in advertisements, and on television and music videos. "They come into the gym and say, 'Have you seen this guy? He looks amazing.' "

Experts say the self-improvement isn't bad. But a growing number of men are going to extremes, and researchers plan to reexamine treatments for men who are obsessed with their appearance.

Reading Comprehension

1. How good were your predictions?

Prediction	Not Accurate	Accurate
1		
2		
3		

2. If you found the answer to your questions, what were they?

_____

_____

_____

Check the Facts

Check (✓) the questions you can answer after reading once. Then go back and look for the answers you are unsure of.

READING 1

_____ 1. Does the writer believe that concern for appearance is a bad thing?

_____ 2. What are some examples of the advantage that attractive people have in our society?

_____ 3. Do people often think that attractive people are less intelligent?

_____ 4. Is concern for appearance a modern idea?

_____ 5. How is our concept of physical appearance different from other cultures' or other eras' perception?

READING 2

_____ 1. What is the purpose of *Extreme Makeover?*

_____ 2. What happens to people on the program?

_____ 3. How many people apply to be on the show?

_____ 4. How is an *Extreme* makeover different from a regular makeover?

_____ 5. How can you apply for an *Extreme* makeover?

READING 3

_____ 1. Why are women sometimes called the *fair* sex?

_____ 2. What percentage of men are happy with their appearance?

_____ 3. Name three things that men are doing to make themselves more attractive.

_____ 4. Why do men say that they want to be more attractive?

_____ 5. Does Mike Lyons agree with these reasons? Why or why not?

Analyze

1. How does the information in Reading 1 support the main idea of Reading 3?

2. How is Reading 2 different from the other two? Does it support or refute the ideas in Readings 1 and 3? Why or why not?

Vocabulary Work

1. .Explain the difference between the words in each group.

   From Readings 1 and 2:

   apply   applicants

   _____

   _____

   From Reading 1:

   obsessed   obsession

   _____

   _____

   attractive   attraction

   _____

   _____

2. Underline the parts of the words that you know. Then guess the meaning of the whole word.

Word	Reading	Meaning
understandable	1	_____
extraordinary	2	_____
undergo	2	_____
makeover	2	_____
reintroduce	2	_____
appearance	3	_____
attractive	3	_____
self-improvement	3	_____

Guess Meaning from Context

1. Work with a partner. Look back at the readings and try to guess
    the meaning of these words.

Word	Reading	Meaning
vanity	1	_____
extreme	2	_____
motto	2	_____
dying	3	_____
implants	3	_____

2. Then turn to page 165 and match the meanings with the words.

3. Look at the words you guessed correctly. Look back at the readings.
    What clues did you use?

4. Guess what each person does.

    a. plastic surgeon   _____

                             _____

    b. eye surgeon   _____

                             _____

    c. cosmetic dentist   _____

                             _____

    d. hair stylist   _____

                             _____

    e. fashion consultant   _____

                             _____

    f. makeup expert   _____

                             _____

    g. personal trainer   _____

                             _____

Reading Skills

Understanding Cohesion

1. What two words in Reading 2 refer to the people who are on the *Extreme Makeover* show?

   _____   _____

2. In Reading 2, who are the "lucky two"?

   _____

Discussion

1. Do you believe that attractive people have more advantages in our society? Why or why not?

2. Have you ever watched a show like *Extreme Makeover?* If so, did you enjoy it? Why or why not?

3. Do you think that it's better that men are caring more about their appearance? Why or why not?

PART II

This reading is more difficult than the articles in Part I. Read it for the main ideas. Do not worry if you cannot understand everything.

Read It

Read to find the answers to these questions.

1. Why did the researcher go to Kenya?

2. What is surprising about the Maasai people?

3. How do the Maasai judge beauty?

 **READING**

Body Dissatisfaction?
Maybe the Maasai Have the Answer

It is common knowledge that many Americans are unhappy with their appearance. However, do people in other cultures feel the same? Social researcher Robert Biswas-Diener wanted to find out, so he went to Kenya to study the Maasai people.

He conducted his study in a village that had no television, no magazines, or other forms of media. He asked the people questions such as, "How satisfied are you with your physical appearance?" Their answers were surprising. Everyone in the village was completely satisfied! They sometimes said that other people in the village were unattractive, but they had a high opinion of their own appearance.

Why do the Maasai have such a healthy outlook on physical beauty? According to Dr. Biswas-Diener, there are several reasons. One of the most important is that they focus on things they can control,

> . . . every single person I interviewed mentioned jewelry as [necessary] for attractiveness. . . . the Maasai wisely focus on adornment rather than the body itself when trying to appear attractive.

There is also a major difference in the way the Maasai look at their bodies. Out of 120 people that were interviewed, only one mentioned breast size when asked to describe a good-looking woman. Instead, the Maasai talked about cleanliness, white teeth, short hair, height (tall is good), and elongated ear lobes. (Maasai women lengthen their ear lobes by wearing heavy earrings.)

Americans, on the other hand, are obsessed about things over which they have limited control. Plastic surgery, diets, liposuction, face lifts, exercise programs, and breast implants are part of a culture that wants to control all aspects of physical appearance. Americans believe they have more control over their physical appearance than the Maasai do. And they are correct. Technology gives them more control. Ironically, this control makes them feel more dissatisfied.

Perhaps the greatest difference that the researcher found between American and Maasai cultures is the definition of attractiveness itself. In the Maasai language, the word for physical appearance can also be used to describe morality. In fact, the Maasai usually think about attractiveness in terms of both physical traits and moral character. When he asked the Maasai to describe a good-looking person, they often used adjectives such as *friendly, well-respected, disciplined,* and *brave.*

So it seems according to the research that the Maasai are more satisfied with their physical appearance for three main reasons. They focus more on adornment than physical attributes. When they do think of bodily characteristics, they focus on those they can easily change. Finally, the Maasai consider behavior and character, as well as physical beauty, when they think about attractiveness.

Vocabulary Work

Guess Meaning from Related Words

Find new forms of these words in the reading. Guess their meaning.

attractive   _____   _____

satisfy   _____   _____

clean   _____

Idea Exchange

Think about Your Ideas

1. Check (✓) the things that you do now or would do in the future to be more attractive.

2. Put a question mark (?) next to the things you might do.

3. Put an *X* next to the things you would never do.

_____ style your hair

_____ dye your hair

_____ straighten your hair

_____ curl your hair

_____ get hair replacement (for baldness)

_____ use makeup on your face

_____ shave your face

_____ shave your legs

_____ diet to lose weight

_____ exercise to have a better body

_____ have plastic surgery on your face

_____ have plastic surgery on your body

_____ have cosmetic dentistry

_____ get colored contact lenses

_____ pay a fashion consultant

Talk about Your Ideas

1. How important is appearance in your culture? Is it as important for men as it is for women?

2. Do some people go too far to be attractive? If so, how do you define *too far*?

3. For the Maasai, personal qualities are an important part of attractiveness. How important are they to you? Would you go out with someone who was not physically attractive but someone you really liked? Why or why not?

For CNN video activities about beauty and makeovers, turn to page 176.

Lying: What's THAT on your resume?

PREVIEW

Discuss the answers to these questions.

1. Who do you think is more likely to lie?

a politician

a journalist

a religious leader

a salesperson

the president of a company

2. Do you think most people . . .
   - usually tell the truth?
   - lie when it's convenient?
   - lie only if they think they have to?
   - usually lie only about unimportant things?
   - only lie about important things?

PART I

Predict

Skim the three readings and make predictions.

1. Which articles talk about catching liars?
2. Do people lie more on the telephone or in e-mail messages?
3. How often do people lie on their resumes?
4. Do people usually look at you when they are lying?
5. Write a question that you think each article may answer.

_____

_____

_____

Read It

Read the articles and look for the answers to your questions.

 **READING 1**   Resumes: Fact or Fiction?

Exaggeration Is Common, But Risky

People are sometimes "creative" when they are writing their resumes. That doesn't surprise Edward C. Andler. "Cheating on resumes is very common," says Andler. He is a *resume detective* and the author of *The Complete Reference Checking Handbook.* "Many people are getting away with it, so more people are trying to do it."

Andler's surveys show that about one-third of all resume writers exaggerate their background and accomplishments. Approximately 10 percent of job seekers "seriously misrepresent" their work histories. In some fields, such as sales, the numbers are even higher.

Typical lies include fictional degrees, false job titles, exaggerated responsibilities, and the changing of dates of previous employment to hide times of unemployment. Some resume lies, such as fake degrees, are easy to discover. Other lies, particularly exaggerations, are harder to check. "Most companies will only give you dates of employment, and that's it, no details," Andler says.

However, Andler uses other techniques to discover lies on resumes. For example, when he checks references, he asks for the name of another work colleague. A call to that person helps him find untruths. "A person who gives a reference is supposed to say good things. They are prepared and they don't want to be negative. However, when you call another colleague, you often get more truthful answers." Still, many applicants get away with their lies. And that is why so many people continue to do it. "Our message to people who cheat is just don't do it," says Andler. "We may not catch you now, but sooner or later, somebody will."

Need to Lie? Better Make a Phone Call

Whom can you trust? The answer is the e-mailer and not the telephone caller. Jeffrey Hancock of Cornell University asked 30 students to keep track of e-mails, calls, conversations, and instant messages for one week. He also asked them to admit how many lies they told during the week. The results? People admitted lying in

- four out of ten phone calls
- three out of ten face-to-face conversations
- two out of ten messaging series
- one out of seven e-mail strings, although experienced users were more likely to lie more often

These results have surprised psychologists. Some expected e-mailers to be the biggest liars. They thought that people would be more uncomfortable lying when face-to-face. Others expected people to lie more in face-to-face conversations because we have more experience with that kind of communication. But Hancock says it is also important to note whether there is a record of the lie or not. He claims that people are afraid to lie when they know their lies are being recorded. This is why fewer lies appear in e-mail than on the phone.

People are also more likely to lie when they don't have time to think of a response. That is why people lie more often on the telephone or in instant message conversations. He found many lies are automatic responses to an unexpected question, such as: "Do you like my dress?" Hancock hopes his research will help companies work out the best ways for their employees to communicate. For instance, the phone might be the best for sales where employees are encouraged to stretch the truth. But for work evaluations, where honesty is important, e-mail very well could be the best place to have a conversation.

 **READING 3** Don't Be Fooled Again

There is no foolproof way of telling when someone is lying, but there are various signs to look for. For example, liars often touch their faces. A liar may stroke his chin or touch his nose. In fact, the fairy-tale Pinocchio is closer to reality than one might think. According to the Chicago Smell and Taste Treatment and Research Foundation, people's noses get bigger when they lie because more blood goes to the nose. This extra blood causes nasal tissue to itch. As a result, people often scratch their noses when they are lying. The researchers discovered this when they watched a tape of a person who was lying. When the person was telling the truth, he didn't touch his nose. When he was lying, he touched it once every four minutes.

You should also watch a person's eye movements. Most people think that we maintain eye contact when we tell the truth and look away when we lie. That's not true. Many people actually look right at you when they are lying. Liars consciously try to look at you because they want to appear sincere. However, there is an unconscious reason why people don't look at you when they are telling the truth. When people have to retrieve information from memory, their eyes move up. They do this unconsciously, but consistently.

The point here is not that any particular behavior means that a person is lying. The secret is to watch people closely and follow their mental processes. Look for their patterns and see when their behavior changes. Watch for an answer that breaks the rules—the odd one out will be the lie. Now that you know how this works, go out and try it with friends and family. Challenge them to lie convincingly as you watch their eye movements and body language. The more you practice detecting lies, the better you'll get.

Reading Comprehension

Check Your Predictions

1. How good were your predictions?

Prediction	Not Accurate	Accurate
1		
2		
3		
4		

2. If you found the answers to your questions, what were they?

_____

_____

_____

Check the Facts

Write *true* (T) or *false* (F). Then go back and look for information to correct the statements that are false.

READING 1

_____ 1. People are often untruthful on their resumes.

_____ 2. People never lie about college degrees.

_____ 3. A lie is more difficult to check than an exaggeration.

_____ 4. People who write references are usually truthful.

_____ 5. It can be dangerous to lie on your resume.

READING 2

_____ 1. Jeffrey Hancock did research on resumes.

_____ 2. People lie more often on the telephone than in e-mail messages.

_____ 3. People lie more often in face-to-face conversations than on the telephone.

_____ 4. People probably lie less in an e-mail because it is written communication.

_____ 5. When people don't have time to think of an answer, they usually tell the truth.

In which picture or pictures is the woman telling a lie? Why do you think so?

1.  2.  3.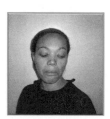

Analyze

1. Would the information in Reading 3 be useful to the researchers in Reading 2? Why or why not?

2. One of the conclusions of the researchers in Reading 2 is inconsistent with the information in Reading 1. What is it? Why is it inconsistent?

3. How could an employer use the information in Reading 3?

Vocabulary Work

Guess Meaning from Context

1. Check (✓) the words that refer to lies or lying. Circle the nouns. Underline the verbs once. Draw two lines under the adjectives.

   ___ accomplishments

   ___ automatic

   ___ cheating

   ___ fake

   ___ false

   ___ fictional

   ___ get away with it

   ___ misrepresent

   ___ sincere

   ___ untruthful

   ___ untruths

Guess Meaning from Related Words

1. Underline the parts of the words that you know. Then guess the meaning of the whole word.

Word	Reading	Meaning
misrepresent	1	_____
untruths	1	_____
background	1	_____
foolproof	3	_____
convincingly	3	_____

2. Explain the differences among these related words.

exaggeration   exaggerating   exaggerated   exaggerate

_____

consciously   unconsciously   unconscious

_____

employment   unemployment

_____

fiction   fictional

_____

Reading Skills

Identifying Euphemisms

A <u>euphemism</u> is a mild, indirect, or vague word that we sometimes use instead of a word that is direct or offensive. Euphemisms sometimes have quotation marks. Which of the underlined words and phrases are euphemisms? What are they euphemisms for?

1. People are sometimes "<u>creative</u>" when they are writing their resumes.

2. Others expected people to lie more in <u>face-to-face</u> conversations . . .

3. . . . employees are encouraged to <u>stretch the truth</u>.

Discussion

1. Do you think that it's bad to exaggerate on your resume? When does an exaggeration become a lie?

2. Do you find it easier to lie on the telephone than in other situations? If so, why?

3. Can you tell when people are lying to you? How?

PART II

This reading is more difficult than the articles in Part I. Read it for the main ideas. Do not worry if you cannot understand everything.

Read to find the answers to these questions.

1. What two different messages do we get about lying?

2. Who lies about their past?

3. Are married couples more or less honest than people who are dating?

4. Why did the student have to stop his research about lying?

5. What are "white lies"?

  READING   Living with Lies

Social psychologists say we're all liars and that's OK.

   Many people believe that used car salesmen and politicians are more untrustworthy than the rest of us, but studies show that lying is very common in all professions and levels of society. Leonard Saxe, professor of psychology at Brandeis University, points out that most of us receive many different messages about lying. Although parents and teachers tell us that it's always better to tell the truth, society often rewards deception. For example, if you arrive late for a meeting, you'll probably be in a lot of trouble if you say that you overslept. However, if you lie and say there was a lot of traffic, everyone will understand. Furthermore, lying is actually necessary in many occupations. Reporters lie to get stories. Police officers lie to make people confess. And lawyers think up incredible stories to help their clients.

People also lie about their accomplishments. In recent years, a number of well-known people—from coaches and business executives to college professors and journalists—have admitted that they have lied about their pasts. Many research psychologists say that we should not quickly criticize such people because most of us lie in the same ways at times. "Each of us creates our own personal myth—our own story about ourselves," Ford says. That story often exaggerates some facts while leaving out others.

Dishonesty is also very common in romantic relationships. According to Dory Hollander, psychologist and author of *101 Lies Men Tell Women,* 85 percent of the couples interviewed in a 1990 study of college students reported that one or both partners had lied to each other. Bella DePaulo, a psychologist at the University of Virginia, also found that dating couples lie to each other about 33 percent of the time—perhaps even more often than they lie to other people. Fortunately, husbands and wives are not as deceptive. Spouses lie to each other in about ten percent of their major conversations.

Researchers argue that in some cases telling lies actually helps us connect with other people. DePaulo argues that some lying is necessary in everyday life. "It would be a disaster if everybody were totally honest," she says. She reported an experiment in which one of her students tried to avoid telling lies for several weeks. The task was so difficult that the student was unable to complete his research and had to apologize to a lot of people afterward.

Certain cultures may place special importance on *white lies.* (A *white lie* is a lie about a very unimportant matter or one that is meant to avoid hurting the listener's feelings.) A survey showed that only about half of Korean Americans believe that doctors should not tell patients the truth if they are dying. In contrast, nearly 90 percent of Americans of European or African descent felt that the patients should know the truth.

It's also not surprising that research shows that we are more likely to tell white lies to people we are close to. This is especially true of women. Although the sexes lie with equal frequency, women are especially likely to lie in order to protect someone's feelings. Men, on the other hand, more often lie about themselves.

Everyone who believes that lies are always bad should think about what would happen if we always told the truth. It might seem like the world would be a better place. On the other hand, all that honesty might destroy our ability to connect with others. Let's face it—lying often makes our social lives easier. Continual lying is clearly a problem, but would we really want to get rid of all of our lies?

Vocabulary Work

Guess Meaning from Related Words

Underline the parts of the words that you know. Then guess the meaning of the whole word.

1. overslept   _____

2. untrustworthy   _____

3. incredible   _____

4. dishonesty   _____

5. well-known   _____

6. continual   _____

Guess Meaning from Context

Work with a partner. Try to guess the meaning of these words. What clues did you use?

1. confess   _____

2. point out   _____

3. myth   _____

4. leave out   _____

Reading Skills

Recognizing Transition Words and Phrases

Find these words and phrases in the reading.

however	furthermore	in contrast	on the other hand

Which ones signal . . .

*   a contrasting idea?   _____

*   when two ideas are contrasted?   _____

*   an additional idea?   _____

*   when an additional idea is coming?   _____

Idea Exchange

Think about Your Ideas

Use the chart to decide if or when you would lie.

Would you lie if . . .	Definitely	Probably	Probably not	Absolutely not
you hated your friend's new haircut?				
a person you didn't like invited you to a party?				
an acquaintance asked you about your salary?				
a classmate asked you to evaluate his essay? (It was terrible.)				
you forgot your mother's birthday?				
a friend asked you if you want her special chicken soup recipe? (It tastes awful.)				
an acquaintance served you steak for dinner? (You're a vegetarian.)				
an employer called and asked you about a colleague? (She is not a good worker.)				
your doctor asks you if you took your medicine? (You didn't.)				

Talk about Your Ideas

1. A proverb from the country of Senegal says, "Lies that build are better than truths that destroy." Do you agree? Why or why not?

2. Have you ever lied and then regretted it? Have you ever told the truth and then regretted it?

For CNN video activities about lying in business, turn to page 177.

CHAPTER

Intelligence: How important is it?

PREVIEW

Discuss the answers to these questions.

1. How important is it to be intelligent? Is intelligence necessary for success? For happiness?

2. Is it possible to be *too intelligent?*

3. Do highly intelligent people have more problems or fewer problems than people with average intelligence?

PART I

Predict

Skim the three readings and make predictions.

1. What do you think the word *dunce* means in Reading 1?
2. What percentage of the population are geniuses?
3. Why are geniuses lonely?
4. Write a question for each reading.

_____

_____

_____

Read It

Read the article and look for the answers to your questions.

 READING 1   What's Better: A Dunce or a Genius?

A *dunce*, which means a very stupid person, is an eponymous term—a word that comes from someone's name. In this case, the person was John Duns Scotus. He was a thirteenth-century philosopher. Duns was not really stupid, but he had some strange ideas. Although he was very respected in his time, other philosophers began to criticize him after he died. His followers, the *dunsmen*, were fanatical believers in his ideas. They refused to give them up and people began to laugh at them. And so, *dunce* came to mean *idiot*.

The dunce cap also came from John Duns. He believed that conical hats increased learning. His theory suggested that knowledge is centralized at the point of the cone and then funneled down into the brain of the wearer. People soon realized that this was an idiotic idea. So the *duns cap* became a symbol of stupidity.

However, being a dunce isn't all bad. There are a lot of famous people that seemed like dunces to their teachers.

- Albert Einstein couldn't read until he was seven.
- Isaac Newton did poorly in grade school.
- When Thomas Edison was a boy, his teachers told him he was too stupid to learn anything.
- Leo Tolstoy flunked out of college.
- Wernher von Braun (father of the U.S. space program) failed ninth-grade algebra.
- Louis Pasteur got a C in chemistry in college.

More recently, Bill Bradley, a former U.S. senator, got a very low score on his college entrance examination. He scored only 485 out of a possible 800, yet he became a Rhodes scholar and a well-known lawmaker. These men prove that children who are slow starters, students who get poor grades, and people who don't do well on tests may do very well in life.

On the other hand, there are geniuses who are absolute failures outside the classroom. For example, Theodore Kaczynski, better known as "The Unabomber," was no dunce at all. He skipped two years of high school, graduated from Harvard, and got a Ph.D. in math. After graduating he was unable to cope with the outside world, and he went insane. He moved to Montana to live alone and started sending letter bombs to people he didn't know. I'd much rather live in a country run by *dunces* such as Albert Einstein and Bill Bradley than by geniuses like Theodore Kaczynski.

READING 2   IQ Scores and Population

Your IQ is your score on a particular intelligence test. The test has an average score of 100 points. That means if your IQ is 100, half of the population scores higher than you. The other half scores lower than you. If you have an IQ of 130, 97.5 percent of people in your age group scores lower than you. Only 2.5 percent scores higher. The following is a graph of IQ scores for an entire population.

IQ Range

85–114	Average
115–124	Above average
125–134	Gifted
135–144	Highly gifted
145–164	Genius
165–179	High genius
180–200	Highest genius
>200	"Unmeasurable" genius

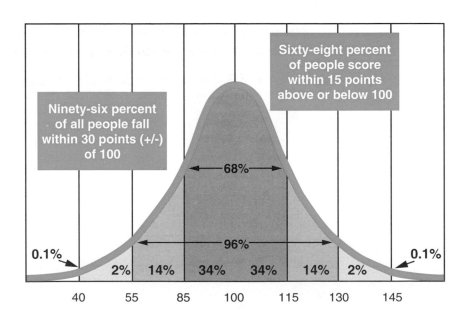

READING 3 The Loneliness of Being a Genius

Many people think that it must be great to be a child prodigy. You're smarter than everyone—even your teachers. All your friends are jealous because you don't have to work in school. Your parents are really proud of you and they never complain about your schoolwork.

Unfortunately, for most prodigies, the statements above are incorrect. Many child prodigies have lonely, friendless childhoods. Why? Because their intellectual, social, emotional, physical, and chronological ages are very different. Even a very young prodigy may have the intelligence of an adult, but he or she still has the social and emotional level of a young child.

Research on the development of children's friendships shows that friends think of themselves as similar to each other. This means two

children who are friends like the same activities and they act and speak in similar ways. Many highly gifted children can find no one who is like them, so they end up lonely and isolated.

For example, Ian is six. His IQ is over 200, and he is passionate about dinosaurs. Many children of all ages also like dinosaurs. However, Ian rarely finds someone to talk to about his passion. Other six-year-olds know too little. Even older children don't know enough. And they don't find his knowledge interesting. In fact, they often don't like him because he keeps correcting them. Ian can only talk about dinosaurs to knowledgeable adults.

The adults are kind, but he is not their social or emotional equal. He's still a child. Therefore, Ian never feels he has a true friend because no one really shares his interests at the same level.

Reading Comprehension

Check Your Predictions

1. How good were your predictions?

Prediction	Not Accurate	Accurate
1		
2		
3		

2. If you found the answers to your questions, what were they?

_____

_____

_____

Check the Facts

Check (✓) the questions you can answer after reading once. Then go back and look for the answers that you are unsure of.

READING 1

_____ 1. What was John Duns Scotus's profession?

_____ 2. How did people feel about him when he was alive?

_____ 3. How did people feel about his followers after he died?

_____ 4. Why did John Duns wear a *dunce* cap?

_____ 5. Name two famous men that were *dunces* in school.

_____ 6. Why is Theodore Kaczynski famous?

READING 2

_____ 1. What percentage of the population is average?

_____ 2. What percentage is above average?

READING 3

_____ 1. Why does the author feel sorry for child prodigies?

_____ 2. Why do child prodigies have problems making friends?

_____ 3. What happens when child prodigies play with children their own age?

_____ 4. What happens when child prodigies play with older children?

_____ 5. What is Ian interested in?

_____ 6. Can he talk about his interests with other children? Why or why not?

_____ 7. Who can he talk to?

_____ 8. Why does Ian feel that he doesn't have any friends?

Analyze

1. What percentage of the population does Ian fall into?

2. What group is Ian in the IQ scale?

3. Were most of the men listed in Reading 1 child prodigies? Why or why not?

Vocabulary Work

Guess Meaning from Related Words

1. Underline the parts of the word that you know. Then guess the meaning of the whole word.

   lawmaker   _____

   friendless   _____

   knowledgeable   _____

   gifted   _____

2. How are the following words related?

   a. lonely   loneliness   _____

   b. passion   passionate   _____

   c. problem   problematic   _____

   d. cone   conical   _____

   e. idiot   idiotic   _____

   f. stupid   stupidity   _____

Guess Meaning from Context

1. Work with a partner. Look back at the readings and try to guess the meaning of these words and phrases.

Word	Reading	Meaning
absolute	1	_____
eponymous	1	_____
child prodigy	3	_____
chronological	3	_____
genius	1/ 2/ 3	_____
fanatical	1	_____
flunked out of	1	_____
jealous	3	_____

2. Then turn to page 166 and match the meanings with the words.

3. Look at the words you guessed correctly. Look back at the reading. What clues did you use?

4. How intelligent is *too* intelligent? Why?

Reading Skills

Finding Main Ideas

1. Which statement is the main idea in Reading 1?

    a. John Duns was a stupid man.

    b. Many famous people are stupid.

    c. Success in school does not necessarily mean success in life.

2. Where is the main idea stated?

3. What is the main idea of Reading 3?

    a. Being a child prodigy can cause social problems.

    b. Child prodigies are more intelligent than other children.

    c. Many people don't like child prodigies.

Discussion

1. Do you know anyone who is very intelligent? Do they have the kinds of problems described in Reading 3?

2. Do you know anyone who doesn't do well in school but is very successful outside of school?

PART II

This reading is more difficult than the articles in Part I. Read it for the main ideas. Do not worry if you cannot understand everything.

Read It

Read to find the answers to these questions.

1. What is an *autistic savant?*
2. Are autistic savants good at seeing details or the big picture?
3. How does Snyder define creative ability?
4. How does his machine work?

 READING

Scientist Invents Creativity Machine

Sydney, Australia—Scientist Allan Snyder thinks that he has invented a machine to make people more creative. Actually, he says that his machine will make people more like *autistic savants*. *Autistic savants* are people who are mentally disabled but they have one remarkable

(Continued on page 124)

ability. They can be calendar calculators (able to tell you the day of the week for any date in history); musical savants (able to play a complex piece after hearing it only once), or even accomplished visual artists.

The director of the Australian National University and Sydney University's Centre for the Mind says that his machine sends out magnetic signals. The signals stop part of the brain from working so that we can see things in greater detail. He believes that this is the key to the amazing abilities of autistic savants. But their problem is that they can't turn this ability off.

Creativity requires being able to see the details of a situation or idea, as well as the big picture, he says. However, most of us only see the big picture. For instance, if we read a book, we will probably remember what the story was about, but not particular words and passages.

Autistic savants see the detail, rather than the whole. However, for the rest of us, we try to fit the things we see and hear into the big picture in our brains. Snyder believes that creativity machines might eventually be a valuable tool in schools. "The biggest block to learning is that we only see what we know," he says.

In order to make different connections, we have to let go of the big picture—at least temporarily. Snyder says the strategy could help adults speak a second language without an accent and to improve their memory for details.

He defines creativity as being able to make connections between ideas that seem unrelated. In order to make these connections, we have to begin to see situations in a "nonautomatic way." "This is the power—and the promise—of the creativity machine," he says. Snyder argues we all have the ability to become creative. That is why he is not claiming his machine can turn people into geniuses. However, he believes that it might well reveal the genius that is inside a person, underneath layers of automatic thoughts, speech, and actions.

Vocabulary Work

Guess Meaning from Context

Look back at the reading. Guess the meanings of these words and phrases.

1. remarkable _____

2. accomplished _____

3. mentally disabled _____

4. temporarily _____

5. unrelated _____

6. nonautomatic _____

Reading Skills

Finding Main Ideas

1. What is the writer's main point?

   _____

2. What does he use to support his point?

   _____

Idea Exchange

Think about Your Ideas

1. Circle the correct statement and complete the sentences.

   I'm smarter than most people I know.

   I'm about as smart as most people I know.

   Most people I know are smarter than I am.

   This has helped me because   This has hurt me because

   _____   _____

   _____   _____

   _____   _____

   _____   _____

2. Check your ability level.

	writing	math	art	music	science	languages	other
excellent							
above average							
average							
below average							

Talk about Your Ideas

1. Are you satisfied with your intelligence? Why or why not?

2. Would you like to be really good at one thing and not good at all at most others? Or would you rather be average in many areas?

3. Would you be a test subject in Dr. Snyder's experiments? Why or why not?

For CNN video activities about intelligence, turn to page 178.

Chapter 11

CHAPTER **12**

Graffiti:
You call this ART?

PREVIEW

Which of these do you think is art? Why? Discuss your answers.

PART I

Predict

Skim the three readings and make predictions.

1. Which article or articles give the writer's opinion?
2. Which article comes from a tourist brochure?
3. Which article or articles include direct quotations?
4. Which article or articles are in favor of graffiti?
5. Write a question that you think each article may answer.

    1A. _____

    1B. _____

    2. _____

    3. _____

Read It

Read the articles and look for the answers to your questions.

 (READING 1A)

Photograph a "Big Mistake"

Dear Editor:

    The *Valley Times* made a big mistake when it published the picture of graffiti last Saturday. Graffiti is illegal in Grandview. Graffiti is not art; it's simply vandalism that the public is forced to look at and taxpayers and homeowners have to pay to remove. It is done by self-centered people who don't care about anybody else's rights. The only purpose of graffiti is for people to see it. So, you really helped the vandals when you printed it in your 20,000 papers. What a wonderful surprise for the criminal who calls himself an artist! He couldn't have bought that kind of publicity, but you gave it to him for free. He's probably only sorry that he can't admit publicly that he did it because the police would arrest him.

Gerald Kesner
Grandview Business
Owners' Association

READING 1B

Saturday, September 12
11:00 A.M.
Graffiti Bus Tour Seminar 1: Writing Urban Space

This tour focuses on graffiti art of downtown Los Angeles, MacArthur Park, and East L.A. Videos will be presented and will include Bob Bryan's award-winning film *Graffiti Verité* and ADOBE L.A.'s *Mexopolis,* as well as short clips from *Los Niños de Piru,* Raul Velasquez's *Sabado Gigante,* and others. At Belmont Tunnel and other locations, L.A.'s graffiti artists featured in Bryan's video will discuss pieces that are currently visible.

 READING 2   Graffiti: Art or Annoyance?

Jason Brando is an artist. His work is controversial—not because of its subject but because of where he does it. Jason's obsession is graffiti—a bold modern form of expression. His graffiti art annoys many people because it is very similar to ordinary graffiti that costs cities around the country $7 billion annually in cleanup costs. The city of Harrison alone spends $200,000 a year to rid its public spaces of graffiti. "One act of graffiti leads to more," said Linda Keller, executive director of *Keep Harrison Beautiful,* a civic group dedicated to keeping the city attractive and clean. "It eventually destroys the community."

Marking or painting someone else's property without permission is against the law. Do it and you have committed a crime. You may have to go to jail *and* pay a heavy fine. Brando understands this because he and friends have gotten into trouble with the police more than once. Now when he wants to paint, he goes to a *legal* concrete wall—a wall that has been designated by the city for use by graffiti artists. These walls are scarce in Harrison. Consequently, they are covered with art. Brando must first erase the pictures on the wall with a gallon of cheap paint. This erasure is called *buffing out.* When he is finished, Brando starts painting. Some of his designs contain faces or objects, but most are complicated combinations of letters. They are shaded and colored to look three-dimensional and are quite large.

Brando, who signs his works "Jaser," is considered one of Harrison's best graffiti artists. He works quickly, and he also works big. A typical design is 12-by-7-feet and takes him three hours.

If he's lucky, his works may last two or three days. "Graffiti is a temporary art form. Other people destroy it. Some throw house paint on it or write their names on it," Brando said. "That's why when I'm finished I photograph it. In a few days the photograph is all I'll have."

 READING 3   People Just Don't *Get* Graffiti

Don Yaeger is one of the nine graffiti artists who have contributed to the murals at the new Teen Center. Yaeger recently talked about graffiti art with one of our reporters.

Reporter: It seems that this art form has many different styles.

Yaeger: We all have our individual styles. But it's not necessarily the art form, it's more the medium that's important to us. You have freedom to use the medium however you want to.

Reporter: Do you consider this an art form, even though the medium is most important?

Yaeger: I don't really consider anything an art form. To me, it's all different mediums. I've done all different things. I've done tattoos. I draw with pen and ink. I paint with cans. I paint with brushes. I think of myself as an artist, but I don't want to be called a *graffiti artist* or a *graphic designer.* I work with whatever I feel like at the moment.

Reporter: What do people misunderstand most about graffiti art?

Yaeger: Honestly, you can never understand it unless you step into our shoes and do it. You just really can't. Most people just don't get graffiti.

Reporter: But how are people supposed to react if they don't have that experience and they don't like what they see?

Yaeger: That's OK. Some people don't like Michelangelo's *David.* I'm not going to try to convince them. That's cool.

Reporter: But what about when that attitude becomes public policy? In cities like Philadelphia, they have bus tours for graffiti art, but in Hillsboro some people in power don't seem to like this sort of thing and would rather see it go away.

Yaeger: That's why, before I started to paint, I talked to people at city hall. Their definition of graffiti art was "If it was done with permission, it is art. If not, it's graffiti."

Reporter: But where does that leave the young person who wants to tag and does it on public walls. Is that absolutely wrong?

Yaeger: It's against the law. I'm not going to say it's moral or immoral. It's against the law, and I respect that—that's cool. But there's a lot of things that I don't think should be against the law that are.

Reading Comprehension

Check Your Predictions

1. How good were your predictions?

Prediction	Not Accurate	Accurate
1		
2		
3		
4		

2. If you found the answers to your questions, what were they?

_____

_____

_____

_____

Check the Facts

Check (✓) the questions you can answer after reading once. Then go back and look for the answers that you are unsure of.

READINGS 1A AND 1B

_____ 1. What mistake does the letter writer think the newspaper made?

_____ 2. Why does the writer consider this a mistake?

_____ 3. What is the writer's opinion of people who create graffiti?

_____ 4. Where and when will the tour take place?

_____ 5. What three things will the participants do on the tour?

READING 2

_____ 1. What does Jason Brando think of graffiti?

_____ 2. What does Linda Keller think of graffiti?

_____ 3. Is creating graffiti illegal in Harrison?

_____ 4. Where can graffiti writers paint?

_____ 5. How long do most graffiti paintings stay up?

_____ 6. How does Brando keep his paintings?

READING 3

_____ 1. Who is Don Yaeger?

_____ 2. What does he think is more important—the style of the art or the medium of the art?

_____ 3. What other kinds of art has Yaeger done?

_____ 4. Does Yaeger paint legally or illegally?

_____ 5. Does he think that graffiti painting should be against the law?

Analyze

1. There is only one person the writer of 1A would agree with. Who is it?

   _____

2. What do Jason Brando and Don Yaeger have in common besides the fact that they are both graffiti artists?

   _____

   _____

3. What have the different places mentioned in the articles done about graffiti art?

   _____

   _____

   _____

Vocabulary Work

Guess Meaning from Related Words

1. Underline the part of the word that you know. Then guess the meaning of the whole word.

homeowners	_____
taxpayers	_____
self-centered	_____
criminal	_____
expression	_____
three-dimensional	_____
typical	_____

2. How are the following words related?

public	publicity	publicly	_____
vandals	vandalism		_____
annoy	annoyance		_____
erases	erasure		_____
moral	immoral		_____

Guess Meaning from Context

1. Work with a partner. Look back at the readings and try to guess the meanings of these words.

    visible   _____

    jail   _____

    fine   _____

    mural   _____

    city hall   _____

2. Then turn to page 166 and match the meanings with the words.

3. Look at the words you guessed correctly. Look back at the readings. What clues did you use?

4. The readings contains special words that are used to talk about graffiti. Special words or language related to an area of interest or work is called *jargon*.

    What does *buffing out* mean? _____

    What does *tag* mean? _____

Reading Skills

Understanding Tone

1. One writer is angry. How do you know? What words or phrases does he use?

    _____

    _____

2. What is the attitude of the two graffiti artists? Are they angry? How do you know?

    _____

    _____

Discussion

1. Is there a lot of graffiti in your town? If so, what do people think of it? If not, are there strict laws against it?

2. Who do you agree with—the graffiti artists or Gerald Kesner? Why?

PART II

This reading is more difficult than the articles in Part I. Read it for the main ideas. Do not worry if you cannot understand everything.

Read It

Read to find the answers to these questions.

1. When did modern-day graffiti start?
2. Where did people first write graffiti?
3. Where did they go after that?
4. What does the writer call the *real graffiti*?
5. When did graffiti end on the subways?
6. Why does the writer say that people write graffiti?

 (**READING**)   ## A Personal History of Graffiti

Twentieth-century graffiti began during World War II. Soldiers across Europe started finding the message "Kilroy was here" from a mysterious individual who wrote it on public spaces. Kilroy's *tag* became synonymous with the *V* ("victory") symbol.

In the 1950s, street gangs began writing graffiti on bathroom walls to help identify themselves and to mark their territories.

Modern-day graffiti started in New York City in the late 1960s. It began with young kids writing their names throughout the city. Slowly it became a global movement that is an important part of the art world today.

When I was just a kid in the 1970s, one of our favorite activities was called *bombing*. (The word *bombing* simply means to cover an area with the writer's *tag* in either ink or paint.) We mostly bombed walls and benches in the parks. First, we used colored markers. Later we started making our own markers and added different inks. Black was the most popular color because blue and red faded. White and purple were also popular. Then we discovered spray paint, and graffiti took on a whole new form.

Soon we found that the park wasn't enough, so we moved into the subways. We wanted the whole city to know who we were. Graffiti writers expanded their creativity by using the subway cars as moving canvases. The simple tags of the early 1970s changed into much larger, more complex productions. Unfortunately, the city of New York never saw graffiti as the official art form of the Big Apple. For years, the police fought a battle against graffiti and those who created it.

Consequently, bombing became a much more dangerous activity, but graffiti artists didn't stop. They took greater and greater risks. They risked arrest, electrocution, dismemberment, and even death. This was the *real* graffiti. Then in the 1980s New York learned how to clean the subway cars permanently. This eventually destroyed NYC subway graffiti forever.

You are probably wondering, "What was the point of writing your name or tag all over the place? Wasn't this a form of vandalism? Wasn't this an illegal activity? How can one claim this destructive act was a form of art?" Art can be visually created, such as with a painting or a piece of sculpture. Art can also be a novel, a piece of music, a film, a play, or poetry. Art does not have to be beautiful to its audience. In other words, it doesn't have to be considered good or valuable. Artists use their creations to communicate ideas, attitudes, and beliefs.

For me, graffiti was a way of expressing my existence. Just like companies have logos and nations have flags, graffiti was my way of saying, "Hey, look world. Here I am!" In addition, just like other art, graffiti sends a message. Writers used the subway canvases to express their thoughts on family, religion, and politics.

Today, graffiti has spread around the world. It is also an accepted art form. Today, we see graffiti imagery on book covers, video games, and in cyberspace.

Vocabulary Work

Guess Meaning from Related Words

1. What word is each of these related to? What can you say about –ous?

    dangerous   _____

    mysterious   _____

    synonymous   _____

2. Find a different form of

    risks   _____

    create   _____

    exist   _____

Guess Meaning from Context

1. What can you say about the words in this sentence even if you don't know their exact meaning?

    They risked arrest, electrocution, dismemberment, and even death.

2. What is the meaning of *saw* in the following sentence?

    ". . . the city of New York never saw graffiti as the official art form of the Big Apple."

3. Guess the meaning of these words. Explain the clues that you used.

    a. *. . . using the subway cars as moving* <u>canvases</u>.

    b. *Companies have* <u>logos</u> *and nations have flags.*

    c. *". . . official art form of the* <u>Big Apple</u>.*"*

Reading Skills

Identifying Transition Words and Phrases

This reading is organized in time or chronological order. Find as many of the words and phrases that the writer uses to help the reader understand the order and the time of the events. There are more than ten.

Idea Exchange

Think about Your Ideas

Choose the best four responses to graffiti you think a government should make.

_____ place restrictions on the sale of aerosol paint

_____ set heavy fines and possible time in jail for offenders

_____ make graffiti writers wash off their work

_____ ignore the problem

_____ give rewards to people who report graffiti writers

_____ educate children about why graffiti is bad

_____ provide special walls for graffiti artists

_____ paint all government buildings with special washable paint

_____ other _____

Talk about Your Ideas

1. What can governments do to stop young people from writing graffiti?
2. Do you think that graffiti is art? Why or why not?

For CNN video activities about graffiti, turn to page 179.

CHAPTER

CHILD LABOR: WHO MADE YOUR SNEAKERS?

PREVIEW

Discuss the answers to these questions.

1. Everyone knows that child labor is generally very cheap. Why is it so cheap?

2. At what age are children allowed to work in your country? What kinds of jobs can they have?

3. Did you work before you finished high school? What kind of job did you have? What did you do with the money you earned?

PART I

Predict

Skim the three readings and make predictions.

1. Match the readings to these titles:

    A Child Hero

    Uniting Help for Children

    Children Pay High Price for Cheap Labor

2. Which readings probably have a negative view of child labor?

    Readings 1 and 3

    Readings 2 and 3

    Readings 1, 2, and 3

3. Which reading discusses carpet making in particular?

    Reading 1

    Reading 2

    Reading 3

4. Which reading discusses different types of child labor?

    Reading 1

    Reading 2

    Reading 3

5. Write a question that you think each article may answer.

    _____

    _____

    _____

Read It

Read the articles and look for the answers to your questions. Label each reading with the correct title from page 140.

READING 1 _____

When Iqbal Masih was four years old, his desperately poor, uneducated parents sold him to a carpet maker for $200. For six years, Iqbal made carpets every day. He did not eat well and spent 14 hours a day bending over a carpet loom. As a result, he was tiny and his bones did not grow correctly. The dust in the air damaged his lungs.

When Iqbal was ten, Ehsan Ulla Khan, founder of the Bonded Labor Liberation Front (BLLF), freed Iqbal. Kahn founded BLLF in 1988 to fight against child labor in Pakistan. The organization has freed more than 30,000 children and runs its own schools.

Iqbal went to school and then eventually joined the BLLF to work in support of Pakistan's twelve million child laborers. Although sickly and small, Iqbal was intelligent and brave. As a worker with the BLLF, he spoke to children about their rights and worked to free as many as 3,000 children. He also traveled to the United States and Europe as an international spokesman for the BLLF. On these trips he made speeches asking for an end to bonded child labor. He also asked people not to buy Pakistani carpets because almost all of them were made by children.

Iqbal became an international hero. In 1992, Pakistani carpet exports dropped for the first time in decades. Exports decreased further in 1993 and 1994. Although Iqbal was still a young child, he became the enemy of Pakistan's carpet makers.

On April 16, 1995, the carpet makers got their revenge. Iqbal was shot and killed while riding his bicycle with a friend. His killers have not yet been caught. However, the work of this brave young man continues and the outrage against child labor is growing all over the world.

READING 2 _____

Some work from six in the morning until seven at night for less than 20 cents a day.

Children around the world work to help their families. Millions of them work in ways that are not harmful. But millions more are little more than slaves. Some of these children are only six or seven years old. Often they work 12 to 16 hours a day. They work in sweatshops, mines, garbage dumps, or on the street. These jobs are not only dull, repetitive, and dangerous, they often make normal physical and mental development impossible.

Many child laborers work in the export industries of developing countries. Their stories are often horrific. In one small carpet factory in Asia, children as young as five work from six in the morning until seven at night for less than 20 cents a day. In a clothing factory, nine-year-olds work around the clock for three days straight. They have only two one-hour breaks when they are allowed to sleep next to their machines. Although the children pay a high price, child labor is incredibly cheap. A shirt that sells in the United States for 60 dollars can cost less than ten cents in labor.

Children pay in a number of different ways: they suffer from poor intellectual and physical development, lung diseases, bad eyesight, and bone problems. In the worst cases, they die. Those who survive often pass these problems onto their own children, connecting poverty and ignorance across the generations.

READING 3 _____

Rugmark is a global nonprofit organization that is working to end child labor in the carpet industry in India, Nepal, and Pakistan. Rugmark inspects factories and runs schools for former child workers.

The Rugmark plan is simple. Carpet makers agree not to hire children. They also agree to allow Rugmark to inspect their factories. In return, they can put the Rugmark label on their carpets. The label proves that children did not make the rugs. It also proves that part of the carpet price is used to help the former child workers. Rugmark carpets are sold in Europe and North America.

Since 1995, Rugmark schools have served thousands of former workers. These schools have high academic standards, and children are encouraged to finish high school. Children over 14 years old can join vocational training programs, which are also financed by Rugmark. Finally, Rugmark tries to reunite the children with their families. Children who return to their families are given four levels of support:

- Support for school fees
- Support for books
- Support for uniforms
- Support for other materials

Thanks to organizations such as Rugmark, the number of child laborers in the carpet industry has greatly decreased.

Reading Comprehension

Check Your Predictions

1. How good were your predictions?

Predictions	Not Accurate	Accurate
1		
2		
3		
4		

2. If you found the answers to your questions, what were they?

_____

_____

_____

Check the Facts

Mark the statements *true* (T) or *false* (F). Then go back and look for the answers that you are unsure of.

READING 1

_____ 1. Iqbal Masih's parents owned a carpet factory.

_____ 2. Iqbal made carpets for six years.

_____ 3. Iqbal was very strong.

_____ 4. The BLLF helped Iqbal.

_____ 5. Iqbal went to work in the United States.

_____ 6. Iqbal worked to help the carpet exporters.

READING 2

_____ 1. All children work in terrible conditions.

_____ 2. Some child laborers have dangerous jobs.

_____ 3. Some child workers are practically slaves.

_____ 4. Child workers get good pay for difficult work.

_____ 5. Child workers often have health problems.

READING 3

_____ 1. Rugmark makes carpets.

_____ 2. Rugmark works for carpet makers.

_____ 3. Europeans want carpets with the Rugmark label.

_____ 4. Rugmark teaches children to make carpets.

_____ 5. Rugmark is active in Africa.

Analyze

1. How are the BLLF and Rugmark similar?

2. How are they different?

3. Would the Rugmark model work in industries such as agriculture and clothing? Why or why not?

Vocabulary Work

1. Underline the part of the word that you recognize. Then guess the meaning of the whole word.

spokesman	_____
sickly	_____
reunite	_____
development	_____
eyesight	_____

2. Find a word related to each of these words.

Word	Reading	Related word
import	2	_____
repetition	2	_____
horrible	2	_____
intelligence	2	_____

Guess Meaning from Context

1. Work with a partner. Look back at the readings and try to guess the meaning of these words.

Word	Reading	Guess	Meaning
loom	1	_____	_____
founder	1	_____	_____
slave	2	_____	_____
decades	1	_____	_____
revenge	1	_____	_____
inspect	3	_____	_____
label	3	_____	_____
rug	3	_____	_____

2. Then turn to page 166 and match the meanings with the words.

3. Look at the words you guessed correctly. Look back at the reading. What clues did you use?

4. Reading 2 says that children work in *sweatshops, mines,* and *garbage dumps.* Even if you do not know what these words mean, what can you guess about them?

Reading Skills

Identifying Referents

Say what each <u>underlined</u> word or phrase refers to.

Children around the world work to help their families. Millions of <u>them</u>₁ work in ways that are not harmful. But <u>millions more</u>₂ are little more than slaves. Some of <u>these</u>₃ are only six or seven years old. Often <u>they</u>₄ work 12 to 16 hours a day. They work in sweatshops, mines, garbage dumps, or on the street. <u>These jobs</u>₅ are not only dull, repetitive, and dangerous, <u>they</u>₆ often make normal physical and mental development impossible.

Discussion

1. Are there laws about child labor in your country? Are the laws obeyed? Why or why not?

2. Is child labor a *necessary evil* in some circumstances? Why or why not?

PART II

This reading is more difficult than the articles in Part I. Read it for the main ideas. Do not worry if you cannot understand everything.

Read It

Read to find the answers to these questions.

1. What are three factors that contribute to child labor?
2. Why do some people believe that women should not go to school?
3. What is *child specialization?*
4. Why is it likely that every country has had child labor at some point?

 (**READING**) An Analysis of the Problem of Child Labor Worldwide

Children in developing countries work for a variety of reasons. The most common reason is poverty. Children work so that they and their families can survive. Though these children are not well paid, their families are so poor that they still serve as major contributors to family income. For example, children in poor families in Paraguay contribute almost 25 percent to the total household income.

In developing countries, rural-to-urban migration is another cause of the increasing rate of child labor. In the last 40 years, more and more people have migrated from the country to the city. In 1950, just 17 percent of the population of the developing world lived in urban areas. This figure increased to 32 percent in 1988. By the year

2000, it had risen to 40 percent, and it will probably reach 57 percent by the year 2025. Poor families who move to the cities usually do not find enough employment. Moving to the city forces families into poverty, and poverty forces parents to send children to work.

Tradition is another reason why some children work. Traditional roles can be particularly difficult for girls. In some countries, people believe that women won't fit into traditional roles if they become educated. In these places, it's not uncommon for parents to force young girls to leave school in order for the girls to take over household duties or to work outside the home. By working, the girls assist in paying for their brothers' school fees.

Often parents in developing countries assign different roles to their children. This role assignment is called *child specialization,* and it also contributes to child labor. With child specialization, some children in the family go to school while others work. Many times roles are determined by the birth order. Often the oldest boy attends school while younger brothers and sisters work to support him.

Social class separation also contributes to child labor. For example, people of India's lower social class are usually manual laborers. Everyone expects lower class children to have jobs that do not require an education. Therefore, no one worries when they do not attend school. After all, they don't really need education for their role in society.

Studies show that the roles of children differ in developed and developing countries. While children in developing countries make an important contribution to family income, children in developed countries consume more than they produce. The child labor situation changes as the economic status of a country improves. For example, after World War II, the United States experienced great economic development. Many mothers started working outside the home. For the first time in the United States, children used more resources than they produced. Evidence also suggests that the use of child labor may only be one stage in the development of a country. For example, 150 years ago, England had about the same percentage of child workers as Peru and Paraguay have today. It seems likely that as these countries develop, the amount of child labor will decrease.

Vocabulary Work

Guess Meaning from Related Words

1. Underline the word or syllable that you recognize. Then guess the meaning of the whole word or phrase.

   well paid _____

   household _____

   social class _____

   specialization _____

2. Look for the four different forms of develop in the reading. Complete the chart.

	Part of speech	Meaning
develop	*verb*	*to make progress*
developing	_____	_____
developed	_____	_____
development	_____	_____

Reading Skills

Understanding Organization

Four subtitles for the three sections of the reading are given below. Choose and match the correct subtitle with the reading section.

Roles of Children in Developing and Developed Countries
Cultural Causes
Causes of Child Labor
Economic Causes

Idea Exchange

Think about Your Ideas

1. How does each group contribute to the problems of child labor?

Group	Contribution to Problem
governments	
parents	
employers	
consumers	

2. What can be done to control each group?

Talk about Your Ideas

Use your ideas to discuss possible solutions to the problem of child labor.

1. Which group in number 1 above can be influenced most easily? Why?
2. Which group will be the most difficult to change? Why?

For CNN video activities about child labor, turn to page 180.

CHAPTER 14

Infidelity:
Our cheating hearts

PREVIEW

Discuss the answers to these questions.

1. What percentage of couples think that cheating on their husband or wife is wrong?
2. What percentage of men admit that they have had an extramarital affair?
3. What percentage of women admit that they have been unfaithful to their husbands?

Answers on next page.

PART I

Predict

Skim the three readings and make predictions.

1. Which article looks at cheating from a . . .
   a. personal perspective? _____
   b. research point of view? _____
   c. business angle? _____

2. Which article or articles are probably from a newspaper or magazine?
   a. Reading 1
   b. Reading 2
   c. Reading 3
   d. All of them

3. Before reading the first article, think of two reasons why people cheat on their spouses.

   _____

   _____

4. Who is Penelope in Reading 2?

5. Write a question for each reading.

   _____

   _____

   _____

Answer to Preview questions 1–3 on page 151.

> Although 78 percent of couples are opposed to sex outside of marriage, 26 percent of women and 44 percent of men admit to having an affair.

Read It

Read the articles and look for the answers to your questions.

 READING 1   The Hows and Whys of Cheating

Why do men and women cheat on their partners? Experts say that the reasons fall into two main categories. In the first category, the cheaters are unhappy because there's something wrong with their relationship. In the second category, the cheaters want the excitement of having an affair.

How Men and Women Differ

In general, experts say, men are more likely to cheat for the excitement. Unfaithful women, however, are usually unhappy in their marriage. They usually don't look for someone new unless there is serious trouble in their relationship. But things are changing, notes expert Dr. Nancy Glass, "The traditional male affair that was primarily motivated by sex is changing. More men are having affairs with emotional ties. Meanwhile, women are having more affairs for the sexual excitement."

With more men and women working side-by-side, there's more opportunity for strong emotional connections that didn't exist before. "You always had the boss who ran off with his secretary, but now I see many men who are in good marriages . . . who nonetheless form these deep friendships with their co-workers," she says.

Cheating before Marriage

Of course most people think about cheating in the context of marriage, but you can cheat on a boyfriend or girlfriend, too. According to experts, many unmarried couples don't discuss fidelity. This is much more problematic than it was in the past. Twenty years ago, couples waited longer before having sex. When they did start a sexual relationship, both people considered the relationship exclusive. Now, couples start having sex much sooner. And they don't talk about whether the relationship is exclusive or not. The problem usually occurs when one person believes that the relationship is exclusive and the other doesn't.

Is There Hope after an Affair?

"It depends," say our experts. Most marriages survive an affair and many end up stronger afterwards. "I've seen many relationships that were much better after the affair because, up until then, the couple wasn't dealing with their real issues. Dealing with the affair helped them communicate on a much deeper level," says Lonnie Barbach, Ph.D., author of *Going the Distance: Finding and Keeping Lifelong Love.* However, an affair in a dating relationship is also more likely to be the beginning of the end. "Some people cheat as a way of leaving a relationship," says Glass. "They want it to be over, but they can't end it, so they cheat and let their partner get angry and break up with them."

 READING 2

ASK PENELOPE

Dear Penelope,

Janet and I have been best friends for ten years. She has been dating Brad for a year. They're engaged and they're going to get married in two months. Janet is excited and happily planning her wedding. I like Brad, so I was happy at first, too. The problem is last weekend I saw Brad in the park with his old girlfriend. The meeting was not innocent. They were holding hands and kissing. He didn't see me, so he doesn't know that I saw him. Now I don't know what to do. My husband says to stay out of it. But how can I just stand by and watch my best friend get married to a cheater? What do you think? Should I tell her?

Confused in California

Dear Confused,

This is definitely a difficult problem. If you tell Janet, she'll be angry with Brad, but she may also be upset with you. If you don't tell her and she finds out later, she'll be furious with both of you. Either way, it may end your friendship. Since you like Brad, you probably have a good relationship with him. I think that you should talk to him. Tell him you saw him and ask him what is going on. Urge him to call off the wedding if he is unsure about his feelings for Janet. When he knows that you know his secret, he'll probably tell her himself.

Oh, Come All Ye Unfaithful

Two British companies, the Alibi Agency and Ace Alibi, want to help you deceive your partner. They offer customers an alibi for any occasion. Just choose the level of deception you want and these companies will deliver it. For a fee of just $25 to $75 at The Alibi Agency, or a 35-dollar annual membership fee at Ace Alibi, the companies will send you a phony emergency beeper message ("Oh no, It's the boss!") or an invitation to speak at a fictional conference. ("What an honor!") They'll even answer the telephone if your partner gets suspicious and calls the hotel ("Ms. Graham isn't in. Would you like to leave a message?"). And you won't have to worry that the charges will show up on your credit card statement. Neither company uses its real name on bills.

So far, these alibi services are doing well. In the Alibi Agency's first year of business, the company received over 10,000 customer inquiries. Ace Alibi has signed up more than 1,200 members in less than seven months.

You might be surprised who these clients are. Almost one-fourth are not married and 40 percent are women. "The individuals who are using these services probably don't have very good relationships to begin with," says Elaine Blackwell, a sociology professor at Columbia University. "They're probably just using this as a way to get out of a situation they don't want to face."

Strangely, $1.50 from each Ace Alibi annual membership goes to help children of divorce. And though the company's work is lying, its motto, is "Provide. Protect. Preserve." Ronnie Brock, the founder of the Alibi Agency, doesn't feel bad about his business. He says his service saves marriages. "We are protecting the public," Brock offers. "When people ask me how I sleep at night, I tell them, 'Just fine.'"

Reading Comprehension

Check Your Predictions

1. How good were your predictions?

Prediction	Not Accurate	Accurate
1		
2		
3		
4		

2. If you found the answers to your questions, what were they?

_____

_____

_____

Check the Facts

Check (✓) the questions you can answer after reading once. Then go back and look for the answers that you are unsure of.

READING 1

_____ 1. Why do women usually cheat on their husbands?

_____ 2. Why do men usually cheat?

_____ 3. How are things changing? Why?

_____ 4. Why do people who are not married often have problems with cheating?

_____ 5. Can a marriage work after an affair?

READING 2

_____ 1. Is Confused in California married?

_____ 2. Is her best friend married?

_____ 3. What is Confused in California's question?

_____ 4. What is Penelope's advice?

READING 3

_____ 1. Do the two companies in the article help cheaters get away with their lies or prevent them from deceiving their partners?

_____ 2. What kind of lies do they tell?

_____ 3. Who uses their services?

_____ 4. How does Ace Alibi use part of its profits?

Analyze

1. How does Elaine Blackwell in Reading 3 agree with Nancy Glass in Reading 1?

2. Would the experts in Reading 1 agree with Ronnie Brock in Reading 3 when he says that his business is "protecting the public?" Why or why not?

3. What might Blackwell and Glass think that Brad in Reading 2 is trying to do?

Vocabulary Work

Guess Meaning from Related Words

1. Below are words from the readings. Underline the parts that look like other words. Then guess the meaning of the word.

Word	Reading	Guess
differ	1	_____
primarily	1	_____
sexual	1	_____
problematic	1	_____
fictional	3	_____
unfaithful	3	_____
deception	3	_____

2. Guess the meaning of these phrases from Reading 1 by looking at their parts.

hows and whys _____

side-by-side _____

the beginning of the end _____

3. These words have a meaning that is different from their most common meaning. What are their usual meanings? What are their meanings in the readings?

deep (1) _____

face (2) _____

Guess Meaning from Context

1. Work with a partner. Look back at the readings and try to guess the meaning of these words.

Word	Reading	Meaning
couples	1	_____
fidelity	1	_____
exclusive	1	_____
affair	1	_____
engaged	2	_____
innocent	2	_____
deceive	3	_____
alibi	3	_____
phony	3	_____
suspicious	3	_____
charges	3	_____

2. Then turn to page 167 and match the meanings with the words.

3. Look at the words you guessed correctly. Look back at the reading. What clues did you use?

Understanding Two- and Three-Word Verbs

Look back at these two- and three-word verbs. Write another sentence with each one.

1. ran off with (1) _____
2. deal with (2) _____
3. end up (2) _____
4. break up with (2) _____
5. get out of (2) _____
6. call off (2) _____
7. sign up (2) _____
8. show up (2) _____
9. stand by (2) _____

Reading Skills

Understanding Tone

When you speak your voice has a particular tone. Often that tone is neutral, but sometimes it tells listeners how you feel. Your voice can have many tones such as worried, angry, joking, or serious. Writing often has a tone.

The tone of each of the articles is different.
Which one is:

    a. *personal?*   b. *funny?*   c. *academic?*

Underline sentences or phrases that support your answers.

Discussion

1. Do you agree with Dr. Glass on the reasons why men and women cheat?
2. In your culture, is a sexual relationship before marriage usually exclusive?
3. What do you think Confused in California should do?
4. Do you think the two businesses in Reading 3 are immoral? Why or why not?

PART II

This reading is more difficult than the articles in Part I. Read it for the main ideas. Do not worry if you cannot understand everything.

Read It

Read to find the answers to these questions.

1. How does Dr. Glass define a *committed relationship?*
2. How does she define a *love affair?*
3. When does friendship turn into infidelity?

 READING   Why Good Marriages Go Bad

The psychotherapist Shirley Glass, whom the *New York Times* called "the godmother of infidelity," has written a new book: *NOT "Just Friends."* In her book Glass says that many men and women in committed relationships unconsciously start cheating on their partners when their friendships slowly turn into love affairs.

By *committed relationships,* Glass is referring to long-term relationships both between husbands and wives as well as boyfriends and girlfriends. By *love affairs,*

she means emotional as well as sexual relationships. Glass says that the easy availability of friends and possible partners is creating a "new crisis in infidelity." Opportunity is everywhere, she warns.

"We meet desirable, interesting, bright people at work, at class reunions, in restaurants, and on the Internet. . . . It doesn't matter whether we are happily married. In the moment of attraction, we are open to the possibility of infidelity." Why are some people unfaithful when others are not? The answer, she says, depends on a combination of opportunity, weakness, commitment, and values.

Her book discusses her research that emphasizes the possibilities of romantic liaisons at work. Fifty-five percent of husbands and 50 percent of wives who have affairs with work colleagues have never had an extramarital affair before. Also, a study of 55 single women who have had affairs with married men shows that in 30 percent of the affairs, the men had been the women's supervisors.

"One of the reasons I wrote the book," Glass says, "is because I was seeing so many people in good marriages get involved in an affair that began as a friendship." Is she saying that married men and women shouldn't have friends of the opposite sex? Isn't it possible that some people who socialize or eat lunch together really are *just friends?*

"I think that men and women can be friends, but they really need to be honest about the attractions they feel," explains Glass. "A good friendship with the opposite sex has all the ingredients necessary for romance. You like each other, you share a history, and you are good at discussing your feelings."

The boundary between a friendship and an emotional affair is secrecy, says Glass. "It's not infidelity if there's no secrecy. . . . If the relationship is an open book, it is probably a friendship. When people start trying to hide things, the friendship is becoming something else."

Also, Glass says it's important not to discuss your marital problems with anyone who you are attracted to. If you need to talk to someone about problems with your spouse or about issues in your marriage, talk only to someone who is "a friend of the marriage." Conversely, if you have a friend of the opposite sex who needs support or wants to talk about personal problems, let your partner be involved, too.

Vocabulary Work

Guess Meaning from Related Words

1. Find words in the reading that are related to the words below.

    a. commit _____

    b. conscious _____

    c. fidelity _____

    d. secret _____

    e. available _____

    f. unite _____

2. Does each word refer to a *positive* or *negative* characteristic or situation? Why do you think so?

desirable   _____

bright   _____

crisis   _____

Idea Exchange

Think about Your Ideas

1. What are your culture's *rules* about fidelity before and after marriage? Write your ideas.

    _____

    _____

    _____

2. How are *the rules* different for men and for women? Write your ideas.

    _____

    _____

    _____

Talk about Your Ideas

1. Is there a *crisis of infidelity* in your culture? Why or why not?

2. Many cultures have a *double standard* for sexual behavior. For example, societies often excuse men's infidelity, but severely criticize women who are unfaithful. Is this true in your culture? What reasons are given for this double standard?

For CNN video activities about monogamy and infidelity, turn to page 181.

APPENDIX I: Guess Meaning from Context—
Matching Exercises

Chapter 1, Page 6, Guess Meaning from Context, Exercise 2

Match these meanings to the correct word.

Word	Meaning
media	associations
worms	not together
relationships	persuade
separated	small, soft crawling animals with no legs
convince	television, radio, and newspapers

Chapter 2, Page 17, Guess Meaning from Context, Exercise 3

Match these meanings to the correct word on pages 16–17, Exercise 2.

Word	Meaning
fan	not allow
arrest	violence by a crowd of people
riot	call out in a loud voice
injured	break
mob	to seize or hold by legal authority
smash	hurt
shout	a very large group of angry people
ban	a person who likes a person or thing very much

Chapter 3, Page 27, Guess Meaning from Context, Exercise 2

Match these meanings to the correct word on page 26, Exercise 1.

Word	Meaning
controversial	fashionable
in bad taste	not telling the truth
awards	not true
false	excited
cool	something people don't agree about
deceptive	gives a prize to
enthusiastic	not polite

Chapter 4, Page 40, Guess Meaning from Context, Exercise 3

Match these meanings to the correct word from Exercise 2.

Word	Meaning
fit in	similar
alike	a Roman fighter
peer group	male
taboo	financial punishment
feminine	be one of the group
gladiator	people of the same age and social group
masculine	men wear this skirt in Scotland
kilt	forbidden
fine	female

Chapter 5, Page 51, Guess Meaning from Related Words, Exercise 2

Match these meanings to the correct word from Exercise 1.

Word	Meaning
blacklisted	presenter
white-listed	nice
background	a person's qualities or behavior
timing	nicely used or manage
well-controlled	put on a forbidden list
personality	enjoyable
announcer	vocational or mechanical
likable	put on an approved list
pleasing	past education or work experience
technical	doing something at the correct time

Chapter 6, Page 61, Guess Meaning from Context, Exercise 2

Match these meanings to the correct word from Exercise 1.

Word	Meaning
profile	convince
tracksuit	in person
risk	basic facts of someone's life
anger	before
up-to-date	not real name
face-to-face	danger
persuade	current, new
previous	comfortable clothes for exercising
fake identity	strong feeling of dislike or hate towards someone

Chapter 7, Page 73, Guess Meaning from Context, Exercise 2

Match these meanings to the correct word from Exercise 1.

Word	Meaning
moderate	a kind of snake
manage	a Hindu place of worship
criticize	not extreme
tension	the noise a snake makes
temple	run or operate
cobra	stress
hiss	to say someone is bad

Chapter 8, Page 85, Guess Meaning from Context, Exercise 2

Match these meanings to the correct word on page 84, Exercise 1a.

Word	Meaning
accurate	someone who doesn't believe things without proof
confusing	correct
skeptic	puzzling

Chapter 9, Page 98, Guess Meaning from Context, Exercise 2

Match these meanings to the correct word from Exercise 1.

Word	Meaning
vanity	radical
extreme	coloring
motto	something put inside the body for example, to increase its size
dying	pride
implants	saying

Chapter 10

No matching exercise.

Chapter 11, Page 122, Guess Meaning from Context, Exercise 2

Match these meanings to the correct word from Exercise 1.

Word	Meaning
absolute	according to time
eponymous	radical, extreme
child prodigy	a word that comes from a person's name
chronological	an unusually talented or intelligent girl or boy
genius	had to leave school because of bad grades
fanatical	total
flunked out of	wanting something someone else has, envious
jealous	an extremely smart person

Chapter 12, Page 134, Guess Meaning from Context, Exercise 2

Match these meanings to the correct word from Exercise 1.

Word	Meaning
visible	a large painting on a wall
jail	a building for city government offices
fine	prison
mural	financial punishment
city hall	can be seen

Chapter 13, Page 146, Guess Meaning from Context, Exercise 2

Match these meanings to the correct word from page 145, Exercise 1.

Word	Meaning
loom	the person who began an organization
founder	a tag that says where a product came from
slave	to look at carefully
decades	carpet
revenge	a machine for making rugs
inspect	a worker who receives no pay and isn't free to leave
label	tens of years
rug	to do something bad to someone because that person did something bad to you

Match these meanings to the correct word from Exercise 1.

Word	Meaning
couples	having a formal agreement to get married
fidelity	not including others, restricted
exclusive	fool or trick someone
affair	costs, fees
engaged	groups of two people who are married, living together, or dating
innocent	sexual relationship between two people not married to each other
deceive	proof or excuse that a person didn't commit a crime
alibi	faithfulness, loyalty
phony	pure, without sin
suspicious	fake, not real
charges	wary, distrusting

APPENDIX II: CNN Video Activities

CHAPTER 1 *THE REALITY OF REALITY TV*

Think about It

Answer and discuss the following questions.

1. Take a class survey: What is your favorite kind of TV program: reality TV, sitcoms, dramas, soap operas, movies, talk shows, the news, or other?
2. Quickly write down the titles of the reality TV shows that you watch or know about. How many are there?

Understand It

Read the statements below. Then watch the video once or twice. According to the video, which statements are true and which statements are false? Write (T) for *true* and (F) for *false*.

_____ 1. Some network executives call reality TV unscripted programming.
_____ 2. Reality TV is bringing audiences back to cable TV.
_____ 3. Critics generally like reality TV.
_____ 4. Critics feel that some reality TV shows are encouraging good values.
_____ 5. Trista Rehn, the Bachelorette, agrees with the critics.
_____ 6. Trista thinks it isn't easy to meet good people.
_____ 7. Reality TV is less expensive to produce than sitcoms or dramas.

Discuss It

1. Watch the first minute of the video again with the sound off. Discuss the images you see. How many of the images reflect (your own) reality?
2. What do critics mean when they say reality TV turns us into voyeurs or peeping Toms?

Write about It

1. Do you think reality TV is harmless or harmful? Explain your opinion with examples.
2. Think of a new idea for a reality TV show. Explain the rules.

CHAPTER 2 Sports Fans or Foes?

Think about It

Answer and discuss the following questions.

1. Watch the first 45 seconds of the video without the sound. Where do you think this sporting event took place?
2. What acts of violence do you see happening in the video?

Understand It

A. Before you watch the video, read the statements below. Watch the video once or twice. Then circle the correct word.

1. The fans in Los Angeles are happy / angry.
2. The fans watched the game from inside / outside the stadium.
3. Many Belgian / English soccer fans were arrested in Brussels.
4. The British Prime Minister / EUFA wants to ban soccer fans.

B. Read the texts below. Then watch the video again and fill in the blanks with the correct information.

1. ". . . vandalizing a limousine, torching _two_ police cars and a city bus, destroying _____ television satellite trucks, damaging more than _____ cars lined up at car dealerships, and looting _____ furniture store and _____ computer store."

2. "The fire department responded to _____ calls; _____ people were arrested. Police used riot gear and rubber bullets against the crowd, which they estimated at three _____, and which _____ news organizations put at ten _____."

Discuss It

1. Violence between players in games is increasing. Discuss the impact this might have on young people.
2. According to the National Youth Sports Coaches Association the problem of violence in youth sports has been steadily increasing in recent years in the United States. Discuss what you think might be causing this problem.

Write about It

You are a police chief in a big city where sports violence is common. Write a letter to the mayor about how the city can prevent a riot after a game.

CHAPTER 3 SELLING TO KIDS

Think about It

Answer and discuss the following questions.

1. Name two famous people who set fashion trends among kids.
2. Name two products that are marketed to kids.
3. Think of a successful TV advertisement directed at kids. What does it sell?

Understand It

Before you watch the video, read the statements below. Watch the video once or twice. Then circle the correct answer based on information from the video.

1. Tweens are _____.
   a. teenagers   b. kids   c. singers   d. advertisements
2. Famous people influence _____.
   a. food   b. sports   c. tweens   d. advertisements
3. Tween girls are into sports and _____.
   a. clothes   b. school   c. swimming   d. reading
4. Kids want to be _____.
   a. controversial   b. left out   c. helpful   d. cool
5. Marketing _____ target kids.
   a. critics   b. golden groups   c. strategies   d. in-crowds
6. Sixty-five percent of kids help their parents _____.
   a. study   b. shop   c. play games   d. watch television
7. Airheads candy makes children feel _____.
   a. sugary   b. left out   c. harmful   d. hip

Discuss It

1. According to the video, some critics are saying that advertising manipulates kids. Do you think this is true? How?
2. Do you agree with the expert in the video that children shouldn't associate eating certain foods with being cool? Why?

Write about It

Watch TV shows designed for children with the sound off. Describe the commercials shown during the show in detail. What are the advertisers selling? How are they trying to convince the children to buy something?

CHAPTER 4 MEN IN KILTS

Think about It

Answer and discuss the following questions.

1. Do you know any businesses that have a dress code?
2. What are the advantages or disadvantages of wearing a uniform at work?
3. Is there someplace you would not work because of the uniforms they wear? Describe the uniform and explain why you wouldn't wear it.

Understand It

Read the statements below. Then watch the video once or twice. According to the video, which statements are true and which statements are false? Write *true* (T) or *false* (F).

_____ 1. The employees don't like the kilts.

_____ 2. The kilts are uncomfortable.

_____ 3. The owner of the company, Marcus Ross, isn't from Scotland.

_____ 4. Marcus Ross only wears kilts at work.

_____ 5. The carpenters wear shorts under the kilts.

_____ 6. Some people tease the carpenters.

_____ 7. The owner of the company buys the kilts in Scotland.

_____ 8. The kilts cost $60 dollars each.

_____ 9. Girls like guys who wear kilts.

Discuss It

1. Do you think the kilts make Marcus Ross's company less successful or more successful or neither?
2. What's your opinion? Do you think men should wear skirts? Why or why not?

Write about It

Is there pressure in society for people to dress alike or to wear the right clothes? Describe the clothes you see around you.

CHAPTER 5 TIME CRUNCH

Think about It

Answer and discuss the following questions.

1. Take a survey. How many hours a week do you work? How much vacation do you take a year?
2. How satisfied do you feel about your job? Do you feel your employer values your work? Do you feel overworked?

Understand It

Read the statements below. Then watch the video once or twice. Answer the questions based on the information in the video.

1. Which country's workers work more hours: Japan or the United States?

   _____

2. How many people in the United States feel over worked?

   _____

3. How many workers felt they had no time to reflect on their work?

   _____

4. Who feels more overworked: women or men?

   _____

5. Who feels more overworked: baby boomers or Gen Xers?

   _____

6. How many hours a week would people like to work?

   _____

7. How many people work 6-7 days a week?

   _____

8. Name two other things mentioned in the video that make people feel overworked. _____

9. Name two things that overworked employees are likely to do.

   _____

10. Name two consequences for businesses that have overworked employees.

   _____

Discuss It

In your opinion, is it good or bad that people work so much? Explain your opinion.

Write about It

Do you know of any countries that have better work practices than the U.S? Compare the two countries.

CHAPTER 6 INTERNET DATING

Think about It

Answer and discuss the following questions.

1. What do you think are the best ways of meeting people?
2. Do you belong or have you ever belonged to an Internet dating service? What has your experience been like?

Understand It

Read the statements below. Then watch the video once or twice. According to the video, which statements are true and which statements are false? Write *true* (T) or *false* (F).

_____ 1. After September 11th, people thought dating was not important.
_____ 2. More women than men are online dating service users.
_____ 3. Doug Wyllie thinks online dating is competitive.
_____ 4. Men might be more nervous about finding a partner online.
_____ 5. Faith Sedline says Internet dating is scary at first; then you get used to it.
_____ 6. Faith is embarrassed about finding dates online.
_____ 7. Faith and Matt had a lot of physical chemistry.
_____ 8. Doug is still looking for his life partner.

Discuss It

1. Why do more men than women use online dating services?
2. Would you recommend Internet dating to a friend?

Write about It

Choose one of the following topics:

    Internet Dating is a great way to meet new dates
    Internet Dating is a terrible way to meet new dates

Explain your opinion with examples from the video or the readings.

CHAPTER 7 YOUNG ANGRY HEARTS

Think about It

Answer and discuss the following questions.

1. Describe what you feel physically when you get angry.
2. Can you name some characteristics of people who get angry often?

Understand It

Read the statements below. Then watch the video once or twice. Match the sentences based on the information from the video.

_____ 1. If you get angry often, you   a. help control your blood pressure.

_____ 2. People who get angry every day are   b. that you talk about your feelings calmly.

_____ 3. Anger can cause   c. might get health problems.

_____ 4. Deep breathing can   d. at high risk for hardening of the arteries.

_____ 5. Experts recommend   e. your blood pressure to rise.

_____ 6. Researchers were surprised that   f. young adults were suffering from coronary artery calcification

Discuss It

1. According to the video, people who have a cynical view of the world are at high risk for clogged arteries. Why do you think that's true?
2. Do you think some jobs or professions can have a negative effect on health? Explain your answers.

Write about It

Imagine you are a doctor or nurse with a patient who gets angry and has high blood pressure. Write a list of ways this patient can improve his or her health.

CHAPTER 8 *Calling All Psychics*

Think about It

Answer and discuss the following questions.

1. A clairvoyant is somebody who supposedly sees beyond the range of normal human vision. So what might a "clairaudient" be?

   _____ .

2. What percentage of Americans do you think believe in psychics? _____ Check your answer when you watch the video.

Understand It

Read the statements below. Then watch the video once or twice. What are some main ideas from the video? Check all that apply.

_____ 1. Patricia Masters is a professional telephone psychic.

_____ 2. It costs a lot of money to get advice from a psychic.

_____ 3. Ms. Masters gives advice about life.

_____ 4. Readings are confidential.

_____ 5. After September 11th, more people began seeking Ms. Master's help.

_____ 6. One famous psychic was sued and lost all of her money.

_____ 7. Horoscopes are usually accurate.

_____ 8. Callers are looking for answers to big questions.

_____ 9. Callers are skeptics.

Discuss It

1. Think of three to five things you would like to ask a psychic about your life.

2. Pretend your partner is a psychic. Ask your questions. Then switch roles.

Write about It

Problem: A person visits a psychic. The psychic provides incorrect health or financial advice.

Question: Is the psychic responsible for increased illness or financial loss? Write your opinion.

CHAPTER 9 quick fix surgery

Think about It

Answer and discuss the following questions.

1. On a scale of 1–10 (10 = most satisfied), how satisfied are you with your appearance?
2. If you could change things about your face or body, what would they be: bigger eyes, smaller nose, fuller lips, bigger chin, smaller ears, less wrinkles, less fat, bigger/smaller breasts?
3. What famous person do you think has the perfect face and body? Describe that person.

Understand It

Read the statements below. Then watch the video once or twice. According to the video, which statements are true and which statements are false? Write *true* (T) or *false* (F).

_____ 1. The doctor wants to make several changes to the reporter's face.
_____ 2. The doctor wants to change one of his eyebrows.
_____ 3. People don't trust breast implants anymore.
_____ 4. The total cost of surgery on the brows, nose, and chin is between three and five thousand dollars.
_____ 5. Surgery is never risk-free.
_____ 6. No one has ever died during plastic surgery.
_____ 7. The reporter never liked his nose.
_____ 8. The reporter doesn't want to change his nose.

Discuss It

1. In your opinion, is plastic surgery worth the health risks?
2. Who has influenced your opinion about your own appearance? (Examples: family, peers, the media, medical professionals) Explain.

Write about It

Would you rather be very beautiful with your current intelligence or very intelligent with your current looks? Ask your friends and family and write about their answers. Do their answers surprise you?

CHAPTER 10 *The Business of Lying*

Think about It

Think about the following questions.

1. Have you ever cheated on your taxes? Do you know anyone that cheats on his or her taxes?
2. Have you ever been cheated by a company? Describe what happened.
3. Do you know of any well-known companies accused of fraud?

Understand It

Read the statements below. Then watch the video once or twice. Match the sentences based on the information from the video.

_____1. When Barry Minkow was 16
_____2. His company was worth 240 million dollars
_____3. His company
_____4. Barry went to prison
_____5. According to Barry, right and wrong
_____6. Sometimes it's necessary
_____7. Tax evasion has doubled
_____8. In the end, Barry
_____9. Now Barry helps law enforcement agencies

a. means something different in the business world
b. ran into financial difficulty.
c. uncover fraud.
d. since 1990.
e. he started a carpet cleaning company.
f. paid for his crime.
g. when he was just 20 years old.
h. when he was 23.
i. to cheat to get ahead.

Discuss It

1. What does Barry Minkow mean when he says, "Right equals forward motion; wrong is anybody who gets in my way."
2. Do you think Barry Minkow's new company will be successful? Why?
3. Do you agree with Barry when he says all CEOs will be tempted to cheat at some time?

Write about It

David Callahan says we live in a cheating culture. Do you agree? Where do you see or know about cheating? Explain.

CHAPTER 11   Alia's Bright Future

Think about It

Answer and discuss the following questions.

1. If you could be gifted or talented in one area, what would it be?
2. Think of the friends you have now. Do you think you'd have the same friends if you were a genius?

Understand It

Read the statements below. Then watch the video once or twice. Answer the questions based on the information in the video.

1. How old is Alia? _____
2. What is nanophotonics? _____
3. How does Alia describe her intelligence or her "gift"?

   _____
4. Name three things that Alia does really well.

   _____
5. When did Alia first start to read? _____
6. What does Alia have her undergraduate degree in?

   _____
7. Does Alia study all day long? _____
8. Name two things that Alia doesn't like to do.

   _____
9. When Alia moved to Philadelphia, what did her friends do?

   _____
10. Alia wants to be a professor and researcher. What else does she want to do? _____

Discuss It

1. In your opinion, is Alia a happy girl? How might she be different from other gifted children? Explain your answer.
2. What does the reporter mean when he says Alia is "refreshingly fourteen"?
3. If you could ask Alia a question, what would it be?

Write about It

Do you think gifted and talented people should get as much help as mentally disabled people? Explain your ideas.

CHAPTER 12 Graffiti Gallery

Think about It

Answer and discuss the following questions.

1. Have you ever written or painted on public property? If yes, why did you do it? Did you get in trouble for it?
2. What kind of graffiti do you usually see (e.g., drawings, political statements, or foul language)?
3. What is the most memorable piece of graffiti you've ever seen? Describe it.
4. Look at the first 30 seconds of the video with the sound off. Can you guess what is going on?

Understand It

Read the statements below. Then watch the video once or twice. What are some important ideas from the video? Check all that apply.

_____ 1. People have different opinions about graffiti as art.

_____ 2. Everyone feels that graffiti is art.

_____ 3. The exhibit in Milan is about the history of graffiti as street art.

_____ 4. The exhibit in Milan is about famous American street artists from the 1970s.

_____ 5. Most street artists are happy that they are finally getting recognition.

_____ 6. Some famous graffiti artists will be represented at the exhibit.

_____ 7. Many street artists feel that the art at the exhibit doesn't represent them.

_____ 8. One piece was used for the Olympics in 1984.

_____ 9. One piece at the exhibit will be used as the logo for the Olympics in 2006.

Discuss It

Do you think it's a good idea or bad idea to show graffiti in an art gallery? Explain.

Write about It

Describe the graffiti you see in your city. Can you explain the purpose of the graffiti? Do you think this is art or something else? Explain.

CHAPTER 13 CHILD LABOR IN INDIA

Think about It

Answer and discuss the following questions.

1. How old were you when you had your first job? What did you do? Why did you work?
2. How old were your parents and grandparents when they first began to work? Did they attend school?
3. Are your parents' or grandparents' experiences different from your work and school experiences?

Understand It

Read the statements below. Then watch the video once or twice. According to the video, which statements are true and which statements are false? Write *true* **(T) or** *false* **(F).**

_____ 1. Child labor is legal in India.
_____ 2. At least 60 million children work for a living.
_____ 3. Moham Kubar worked for 11 years as a carpet weaver.
_____ 4. His parents sold him to a carpet manufacturer.
_____ 5. He used to work six or seven hours a day.
_____ 3. Moham's parents punished him for trying to leave his job.
_____ 4. India says pressure from the West won't help end child labor.
_____ 8. India says that in order to reduce child labor they need to reduce poverty.
_____ 9. Adults in India have better working conditions than children.

Discuss It

1. Do you agree or disagree with India that pressure from the West won't help end child labor? Explain.
2. Discuss some of the images you saw in the video. How did they make you feel?

Write about It

Write an opinion paragraph in favor of child labor or against it. Support your ideas with examples.

CHAPTER 14 | Is Monogamy Natural?

Think about It

Answer and discuss the following questions.

1. Do you believe that monogamy or having an exclusive sexual relationship is important for society? Why?
2. Do you believe that monogamy is natural for humans?
3. Do you know of any animals that partner for life?

Understand It

Read the statements below. Then watch the video once or twice. Answer the questions based on the information in the video.

1. Are most mammals monogamous?

2. What mammals mentioned in the video have many partners?

3. How long ago did our human ancestors decide to become monogamous?

4. Why did they become monogamous?

5. How many people in the video think monogamy is natural for humans?

Discuss It

1. In your opinion, what helps a committed couple to remain faithful to each other?
2. Guess the percentage of married couples that get divorced. Share your responses with the class. What do your answers say about marriage? What do your answers say about human nature?

Write about It

Make a list of social and economic pressures on married couples. Then, make a list of solutions how couples can survive these pressures.

PHOTO CREDITS

Chapter 1
Page 1: ©Stephanie Cardinale/People Avenue/CORBIS
Page 3, center: ©David Young Wolf/PhotoEdit
Page 3, bottom: ©Thomson ELT
Page 4, top: ©Jim Raycroft/Index Stock Imagery, Inc.
Page 4, center: ©Ron Chapple/ThinkStock LLC/Alamy
Page 8: ©Ron Chapple/ThinkStock/Alamy

Chapter 2
Page 10, center left: ©HIRB/Index Stock Imagery, Inc.
Page 10, center right: ©ImageSource/SuperStock
Page 10, bottom left: ©Photodisc/Getty
Page 10, bottom right: ©Michael Newman/PhotoEdit
Page 12, top left and center right: ©Maxim Marmur/
    Associated Press/AP
Page 13: ©Associated Press/The Denver Post

Chapter 3
Page 21, top right: ©Hemera Photo Objects, VI
Page 21, top center right: ©PhotoLink/Getty
Page 21, top center left: ©Photodisc Green/Getty
Page 21, center left: ©Ryan McVay/Getty
Page 21, center right: ©Steven S. Miric/SuperStock
Page 22: ©ER Productions/Brand X Pictures/Getty
Page 23: ©SuperStock, Inc./SuperStock
Page 24: ©Ron Fehling/MasterFile
Page 30: ©John Foxx/Alamy
Page 31, top left: ©Larry Williams/CORBIS
Page 31, bottom right: ©Paul Barton/CORBIS

Chapter 4
Page 34, top left: ©RubberBall Productions/Getty
Page 34, top center: ©Ryan McVay/Photodisc Green/Getty
Page 34, top right: ©C Squared Studios/Getty
Page 34, center: ©Dynamic Graphics Group/Creatas/Alamy
Page 34, center left: ©Joshua Ets-Hokin/Photodisc Blue/Getty
Page 34, bottom right: ©image100/Alamy
Page 36: ©Warner Bros Pictures/Zuma/CORBIS
Page 42, top left: ©Michel Euler/Associated Press/AP
Page 42, bottom right: ©Peter Adams/Photographers' Choice/Getty

Chapter 5
Page 44, bottom left: ©Banana Stock/Alamy
Page 44, bottom right: ©Big Cheese Photo LLC/Alamy
Page 45, top right: ©D. Madison/MasterFile
Page 45, top center: ©Keith Brofsky/Photodisc Green/Getty
Page 45, center: ©Mark Gibson/Index Stock Imagery, Inc.
Page 46: ©TRB Foto/Photodisc Blue/Getty
Page 47: ©Associated Press, NOAA
Page 48: ©RubberBall Productions/Alamy
Page 52: ©Bill Varie/Alamy

Chapter 6
Page 56, center left: ©Digital Vision/Getty
Page 56, center right: ©HIRB/Index Stock Imagery, Inc.
Page 56, bottom right: ©RubberBall Productions/Getty
Page 59: ©Image Source Limited/IndexStock Imagery, Inc.
Page 64: ©B2M/Stock Image/Pixland/Alamy

Chapter 7
Page 67: ©ThinkStock/Getty
Page 70: ©Stapleton Collection/CORBIS
Page 76: ©Bonnie Kamin/PhotoEdit

Chapter 8
Page 79: ©Ingram Publishing/Index Stock/Alamy
Page 87: ©James Strachan/Stone/Getty

Chapter 9
Page 91: ©Lucille Khornak/Index Stock Imagery, Inc.
Page 93: ©Reuters/CORBIS
Page 94: ©John Foxx/Alamy
Page 100: ©Yellow Dog Productions/The Image Bank/Getty

Chapter 10
Page 103, center left: ©ComStock Images/Getty
Page 103, center: ©Jeff Greenberg/PhotoEdit
Page 103, center right: ©Ron Chapple/ThinkStock/Alamy
Page 103, bottom left: ©Network Productions/Index Stock/Alamy
Page 103, bottom right: ©BananaStock/Alamy
Page 109, all: ©MC Goodrum Photos
Page 112: ©Richard T. Nowitz/CORBIS

Chapter 11
Page 115: ©Bettman/CORBIS
Page 116: ©SuperStock, Inc./SuperStock
Page 119: ©Associated Press/The Tennessean
Page 123: ©Associated Press/AP

Chapter 12
Page 127, "a": Jan Brueghel, the Elder's "Vase of Flowers"
    (1568–1625): © SuperStock, Inc./SuperStock
Page 127, "b": Andy Warhol's "Campbell's Soup I (Tomato)", 1968:
    ©Bridgeman Art Library, London/SuperStock
Page 127, "c": artist unknown: ©HIRB/Index Stock Imagery, Inc.
Page 127, "d": Alexander Calder's "Flamingo" in Chicago, 1975:
    ©Sandy Felsenthal/CORBIS
Page 135: ©Thomson ELT
Page 136: ©Royalty-Free/CORBIS

Chapter 13
Page 139, center: ©Jeremy Horner/CORBIS
Page 139, right: ©Associated Press/AP
Page 141: ©Associated Press/AP
Page 147: ©CORBIS
Page 148: ©Associated Press/AP

Chapter 14
Page 151, left: ©ImageSource/Alamy
Page 151, center: ©Vernon Leach/Alamy
Page 151, right: ©Widman/f1 online/Alamy
Page 160: ©GoodShoot/Alamy